Pr

As Far As t

"This book is like a door that opens only one way. When you open it, you become more than you were, and there is no going back. These stories will free you to move closer to your own dream of yourself and live more authentically, more joyfully, and more passionately than before. More than just a book, *As Far As the Heart Can See* is an exquisitely written invitation to live your real life."

—**Rachel Naomi Remen, M.D.**, author of
Kitchen Table Wisdom and *My Grandfather's Blessings*

"*As Far As the Heart Can See* is a tonic for the spirit, a series of revelations by way of a series of far-ranging stories as told by Mark Nepo, as only he can tell them: heartfully, honestly, and humbly. Read this book and see how much farther you can see."

—**Phil Cousineau**, author of *The Art of Pilgrimage*
and *The Oldest Story in the World*

"What happens when a poet writes a book of stories about how to live, how to love, how to heal and grow and find our distinct purpose? Here's what happened for me when I read Mark Nepo's *As Far As the Heart Can See*: Each word became a stepping stone on a path through the woods. And not only that: a host of helpers, teachers, cheerleaders, and friends popped off the pages of this charming and wise book to lead me out of the stuck places and into freedom."

—**Elizabeth Lesser**, cofounder of Omega Institute and
author of *Broken Open: How Difficult Times Can Help Us Grow*

"*As Far As the Heart Can See* is filled with stories and guided reflections that not only make us think about life but feel more connected to it. This book can help you access your inner wisdom and caring heart."

—**James Baraz**, coauthor of *Awakening Joy:
10 Steps That Will Put You on the Road to Real Happiness*
and cofounder of Spirit Rock Meditation Center

"Part poetry, part spiritual narrative, *As Far As the Heart Can See* offers us a grounded experience of life seen through a spiritual lens. Mark Nepo invites us into a *sheesh mahal*—a palace of mirrors—where the soul sits on its immortal throne, sparkling like the Kohinoor diamond. Each narrative touches a unique facet of life and draws the reader into reflection—oh soul, look into the mirror of your heart and see with love. See the whole being, the visible and the invisible; the image and the reality; the shadow and the light. This precious book places truth in the core of the heart and shows how pure feelings set it free."

—**Gayatri Naraine**, author of *Something Beyond Greatness*

Praise for Mark Nepo

"Mark Nepo is a Great Soul. His resonant heart—his frank and astonishing voice—befriend us mightily on this mysterious trail."

—**Naomi Shihab Nye**, author of *You and Yours,*
19 Varieties of Gazelle: Poems of the Middle East, and *Red Suitcase*

". . . an eloquent spiritual teacher."

—**Herbert Mason**, professor of history and religious
thought, Boston University, and translator
of *Gilgamesh, A Verse Narrative*

". . . a rare being, a poet who does not overuse language, a wise man without arrogance, a teacher who always speaks with compassion, and an easygoing love-to-listen-to-him storyteller."

—**James Fadiman, Ph.D.**, cofounder,
Institute for Transpersonal Psychology

". . . a great storyteller who has much wisdom."

—*Spirituality and Health* magazine

For *The Book of Awakening*

"Mark Nepo's work is as gentle and reliable as the tides, and as courageous as anyone I've known in looking deeply into the mysteries of the self."

—**Michael J. Mahoney**, author of *Human Change Processes*
and *Constructive Psychotherapy*

"Mark Nepo is one of the finest spiritual guides of our time."

—**Parker J. Palmer**, author of
A Hidden Wholeness and *The Courage to Teach*

"I've been blessed and humbled by reading his words."

—**Marianne Williamson**, author of *Enchanted Love*

For *The Exquisite Risk*

"Mark Nepo's *The Exquisite Risk* is one of the best books we've ever read on what it takes to live an authentic life."

—**Frederic and Mary Ann Brussat**

"A lovely, luminous work that should make a lasting impression on its readers."

—*Library Journal*

"There are books that encourage you to race through from beginning to end, and there are those meant to be savored like a fine meal. Nepo's book is filled with poetic imagery and language, enticing the reader to linger over its delicate flavors. Filtered through his personal experience, Nepo pours wisdom from the chalice of many cultures and faiths."

—*The Cleveland Plain Dealer*

For *Finding Inner Courage*

"Pained by war and aware of injustice in the world, we are in need of wisdom, hope, encouragement. Mark Nepo gives us all of that in this poetic, profoundly thoughtful rumination on how we might live."

—**Howard Zinn**, author of *The People's History of the United States* and *A Power Governments Cannot Suppress*

"What an extreme delight to be engaged with this writing that issues from the heart that thinks and the mind that poeticizes! How rare it is these days to find truly original writing and, even more, thought that has moved way, way beyond and beneath and above the kind of spectator consciousness that characterizes most writing. *Finding Inner Courage* is one of the handful of books I cherish."

—**Robert Sardello, Ph.D.**, author of *Love and the World* and *Silence*

"Anyone interested in improving the global community will appreciate (Nepo's) message."

—*Library Journal*

"What makes (this) book valuable is Nepo's quiet understanding of the constant interplay of surface and depth in our lives, (and) the need to let go of judgments and exercise compassion as we view our own flaws and the flaws of those around us."

—*Publishers Weekly*

"This book is a cornucopia of inspirational stories and insight—a wonderful achievement, an honest and brave book."

—**Robert Inchausti**, author of *Subversive Orthodoxy: Outlaws, Revolutionaries and Other Christians in Disguise* and editor of *The Pocket Thomas Merton*

As Far As the Heart Can See

Also by Mark Nepo

NONFICTION

The Book of Soul

Drinking from the River of Light

More Together Than Alone

Things That Join the Sea and the Sky

The One Life We're Given

The Endless Practice

Seven Thousand Ways to Listen

Finding Inner Courage

Unlearning Back to God

The Exquisite Risk

The Book of Awakening

POETRY

The Way Under the Way

Inside the Miracle

Reduced to Joy

Surviving Has Made Me Crazy

Suite For The Living

Inhabiting Wonder

Acre of Light

Fire Without Witness

God, The Maker of the Bed, and the Painter

EDITOR

Deepening the American Dream

RECORDINGS

The Book of Soul

Flames That Light the Heart (Video Course)

More Together Than Alone

The One Life We're Given

Inside the Miracle (Expanded, 2015)

Reduced to Joy

The Endless Practice

Seven Thousand Ways to Listen

Staying Awake

Holding Nothing Back

As Far As the Heart Can See

The Book of Awakening

Finding Inner Courage

Finding Our Way in the World

Inside the Miracle (1996)

AS FAR AS
THE HEART CAN SEE

STORIES TO ILLUMINATE THE SOUL

MARK NEPO

FREEFALL
BOOKS

Request to cite excerpts from the stories in *As Far As the Heart Can See* can be sent to permissions@threeintentions.com.

Cover image by Mary Brodbeck Woodblock Prints/www.marybrodbeck.com
Author photo by Brian Bankston/www.brianbankston.com

Freefall Books
Published 2020
Printed in the United States of America

Print ISBN: 978-1-7347055-0-8
E-ISBN: 978-1-7347055-1-5
Library of Congress Control Number: 2020907681

For everyone who ever carried a story,
willingly like a seed or unwillingly
like a splinter, needing to plant it
or needing to be free of it.

A story must be told in such a way that it constitutes help in itself. My grandfather was lame. Once they asked him to tell a story about his teacher. And he related how his teacher used to hop and dance while he prayed. My grandfather rose as he spoke, and he was so swept away by his story that he began to hop and dance to show how the master had done. From that hour, he was cured of his lameness. That's how to tell a story.

—Martin Büber

Contents

Staying Close   1

On and Off the Path

Looking and Seeing   9

The Cyclist   13

About to Leave the Earth   17

The Tea Master and the Warrior   21

From Pear to Nest   25

Waiting for the Boat   29

With Great Effort   37

To Sprout an Ear   41

Moses Has Trouble with God's Instructions   45

The Fishermen   49

Unbreakable   53 (Charlotte read this to us.)

The Work of the Worm   57

The Life of Obstacles

The Life of Obstacles   63

A Guide to Rock Climbing   65

Ahimsikha and Angulimāla   69

The Holes of a Flute   77

The Great Awakening   81

The Bridge and the Elephant   85

Abe and Phil   89

In the Mirror   95

Poise   99

Wu Wei's Pot   103

Stories of the Old World   109

Suffering and Loving the World

The Arts of Liberation   115

The Burglar   119

Across the Sea   127

The Great Russian Dancer   129

Hill Where the Lord Hides   133

The Painter is Painted   137

Two Monks Climb a Mountain   141

Suffering and Loving the World   145

Pierrot in the Dead City   153

The Wolf of Gubbio   161

The Falcon of Truth   171

Cain and Abel   175

Keeping the Dish Alive   179

The Invitation to Grow

The Invitation to Grow   185

Tu Fu's Reappearance   187

The Desert and the Marketplace   189

Seeds Within Seeds   193

The Translator's Son   199

Crossing Time   203

Wisdom of the Chew   207

Facing a Demon   211

Hands Like Wings   215

Feeling Small   223

The Illumination   227

Blessedly   231

Notes   235

Gratitudes   241

About the Author   243

Permissions   245

Staying Close

S INCE EVERYTHING IS SACRED, staying close to what is sacred is a matter of presence and attention more than travel to some secret place. In essence, staying close is a pilgrimage to the heart of where we are. Since it is we who lose our directness of living, our task is often to restore that freshness of being alive.

Stories help us. They are teachers. They are medicine. They keep us connected to what matters. They keep us awake. This has always been true. And so, *As Far As the Heart Can See* is a book of stories and parables about staying awake and staying close. Each story has a life of its own that simply used me to become known again in the world. And each has some residue of my life on earth, for no story can come through without some taste of the teller.

The idea to assemble these stories and parables came from the workshops and retreats I have been blessed to guide around North

America and abroad. Regardless of the various reasons to gather, all the workshops have been about staying close to what is sacred. Like roots finding water, we always wind up moving toward what sustains us. Many of my readers have kindly asked for these stories, and it was my wife, Susan, who urged me to make them available in such an interactive way. Putting them together has taught me even more about staying close.

Some of these stories are personal. Some have come from dreams. Some have knocked on the door of my consciousness so persistently that I had no choice but to create names and contexts for their pleas. Quite simply and with wonder at what I've found, I am passing them on. They have all been teachers and continue to be so. I invite you to listen to them, to be with them, and to keep telling them. I hope they will evolve and shape-shift for being in your hands. For every story has in its marrow the accumulated voice of all of its tellers and listeners. Ultimately, I hope they will evoke your own stories and your own sense of what is sacred. I hope something here will lead you to ask others about their stories.

The truth is that long before disciplines of knowledge were formed, long before degree programs were certified, the quandaries of living were addressed and carried forward in pouches of wisdom we call stories. This is how a tribe and its elders would pack their questions and pass on their meaning, as if to say, "We have done all we can with this. Now it is your turn."

We often need to tell our stories over and over, not because we are forgetful or compulsive, but because their meaning is too great to be digested in any one telling. So we recount them, again and again, till we can absorb their meaning and learn to love each other on the way.

I have always been compelled by stories. Like most people, I started out as a witness, retelling the episodes of life that would unfold around me. But as life will do over time, what seems so far away and irrelevant is slowly brought very near; and up close, we discover it is essential. In this way, I have come to realize that we are *in* stories more than outside them. We are more like fish in the stream than fishermen sitting in the grass. More like clay formed in the fire than potters poking at the embers. We are singers waiting to be birthed by a song.

This book then is an invitation to be in relationship with deep and life-giving material. The stories gathered here carry seeds of our humanness. They delve into the courage to listen to your own life, the gift of vulnerability, the willingness to experiment and explore your own voice, the abiding commitment to respect your own journey and the journeys of others, and the life skill of working with what we are given. No experience is required, just a Beginner's Mind and Heart. And the willingness to hear one story and tell another. A willingness to keep listening and trying.

How to Use This Book

There is no need to read this book sequentially. You can discover these stories one at a time, like shells along a shore, or string them together as you would beads on a necklace. It is more important to stay in relationship with them. Discuss them with a friend or a colleague or a child or an elder. Leave them for strangers. If moved, sing them to the moon.

After each story, you will find a set of questions, offered to initiate various forms of conversation: questions to reflect on, to journal with and dialogue with, questions to bring back into your life. I am indebted to my friends for the idea of Table Questions. One day after dinner, Jill blurted out "Table Question!" and began to wonder out loud about something that life had brought her. Two hours later, we were deep in sharing stories and learning even more about each other. From that night, every meal with friends is accompanied by a table question. In response, we roll up our sleeves and drop our stories into the sea of life, like oars that bring us a few strokes along.

As with the stories, use the questions you are drawn to. They are not meant to be sequential, but a series of starting points. They are also interchangeable: questions to journal with can be table questions for conversation and the other way around. If any of these stories or questions can be kindling for some light still out of view, ignite them. If you are stirred by your own stories and questions, I invite you to ignore the ones I've offered.

It doesn't matter how, but if you can rub the pulse of life hidden in these stories and your own, even briefly, like a genie's lamp, the sense of what is sacred will show its magic and usefulness. As sheet music is a riddle until played, the stories we carry and stumble through wait to be held and listened to. For beneath all of life's difficulties, we are brought alive and kept alive by holding and listening.

We all have a need for stories that, when heard and retold, reveal stories within stories which bring us, if awake enough, to the one song at the heart of all stories. I'll meet you there.

Want to hear a story?

On and Off the Path

The world is not comprehensible,
but it is embraceable.

—Martin Büber

Looking and Seeing

WE OFTEN LOOK BUT DON'T SEE until something shifts how we experience the world. Then, the basic habit of our understanding is altered: shattered or expanded, broken apart or open, turned upside down or reduced to the beginning. We call this a paradigm shift. We dread and yet need these unexpected moments to return us to the hidden wholeness in which all things are connected. However, these shifts are not something we can teach, but only lift up and share, only understand better over time.

During a critical time in my cancer journey, I was plagued with deciding the next course of treatment. All the options seemed difficult. We had an unusual winter storm that October. While agonizing over what to do next, I remember watching as the heavy storm brought all the colorful trees down. The leaves, no matter how brilliant, weighed the trees down. If the leaves had let go, the snow would have left the trees standing. This was a stark paradigm shift for me. At a crucial time, it helped me to see holding on and letting go differently.

In the movie *Phenomenon* (1996), the main character has a garden that is pestered by a rabbit eating all his vegetables, no matter what kind of fence he constructs. One night, he wakes to a paradigm shift and sees it all differently. He rushes out under the night sky and opens the gate to his garden and waits. Sure enough, the rabbit wasn't trying to get in. It was trying to get out.

The story of St. Paul is an archetype of a paradigm shift. Saul was a persecutor of early Christians until a moment of revelation knocked him off his horse, and he rose as Paul, a devout follower of Jesus. We could say that the experience of undergoing a paradigm shift is like getting knocked off our horse.

Another example is Sir Isaac Newton's legendary experience with an apple falling on his head and how that opened him to the understanding of gravity. So often, as with Newton, we are led or forced to see anew what already exists. Our very personal awakenings are much like this—sudden and perplexing experiences that restore our original sense of being alive.

How we see matters. In truth, our ability to see with our mind and heart is the only window we have on life. It reminds me of my dear grandmother in Kingsbrook Medical Center in Brooklyn at the age of ninety-four. Upon being told on a beautiful afternoon that what she thought was a gray day was just a dirty window, she shrugged and said, "Got a dirty eye, see a dirty world."

Perhaps the work of love is to help each other clean our minds and hearts so we don't keep seeing a dirty world. Perhaps the work of friendship is to help each other break the habits of mind that prevent us from seeing at all. The stories in this section speak to such shifts in perception and to the friendships we encounter as we stumble on and off the path.

The Cyclist

ON THE DAY OF THE RACE, he waited with the others and felt that life was waiting in the hills. He couldn't quite say why, but a blessing was about to happen. As the gun went off, he could hear the rush of all the racers breathing—like young horses in the morning.

He had trained for months, up and down the sloping hills, cutting off seconds by wearing less and leaning into curves. His legs were shanks of muscle. He often said, "It's the closest thing to flying I know."

On the second hill, the line thinned, and he was near the front. They were slipping through the land like arcs of light riding through the veins of the world. By now, he was in the lead. As he swept toward the wetlands, he was gaining time when a great blue heron took off right in front of him, its massive, timeless wings opening just in front of his handlebars.

Its shadow covered him and seemed to open something he'd been chasing. The others were pumping closer, but he just stopped and stood there, straddling his bike, staring at what the great blue had opened by cutting through the sky.

In years to come, others would ask, "What cost you the race?" Wherever he was, he'd always look south, and once in a while, he'd say, "I didn't lose the race—I left it."

JOURNAL QUESTIONS

- *Tell the story of a time when your hard work had an unexpected outcome and what you learned from that experience.*

TABLE QUESTIONS

To be asked over dinner or coffee with friends and loved ones. Try listening to everyone's response before discussing:

- *What does this story say about what we work toward and what actually happens?*

- *What's the difference between "losing the race" and "leaving the race?"*

A MEDITATION

- *Close your eyes, breathe slowly, and imagine something you are working hard to achieve. Notice without judgment which has more energy for you: the process or the goal.*

- *Close your eyes again, breathe slowly, and imagine your hard work without the goal ahead of you or your reason why to do this behind you. Focus, if you can, only on the process you are in.*

- *Close your eyes, breathe slowly, and picture a bird flying without knowing where it's going. Or a cyclist riding with no destination.*

- *Open your eyes and enter your day.*

About to Leave the Earth

W E WERE WAITING IN THE AIRPORT FOOD COURT. It was early, and he was sitting by himself stirring his coffee. I could hear the wooden stick against the Styrofoam. He had a hitch of sudden pain. It was then I saw the growth like a softball on his right shoulder. There were only a few of us, waiting for security, trying to wake up before being carried from the earth.

Maybe it was being half-conscious, almost removed for a while from our lives, quietly chewing like chipmunks before dawn. But he started telling his story as if we all knew each other. He was dying, and it only seemed frightening when he kept it to himself, "The damn thing is too close to my spine to operate, so I've just got to wait." Then he laughed, "But hey, we've had a lot a' practice at waitin' eh?"

He'd pulled back the curtain between us. Now we were warming each other around the fire, the one that never goes out, the one kept going by the pain we throw into it. A kind flight attendant on her way to Japan moved closer, "You just stay positive, sweetheart, that's what my Daddy used to say."

I felt my own history of cancer, of bursting through the pretense that we're strangers. The flight attendant left, and I wanted to speak to him, to tell him that either way he's already aglow. My heart was pounding. Then his flight was called. He was startled, and I knew, recognized, that he heard the call, for a second, as the one into his doctor's office when he was diagnosed, and then, as the one that brought him into chemo. He went more urgently than he had to and left a small bag.

I grabbed it and ran after him, tapped him on his other shoulder, and began to confess, "I too—" He dropped his shoulders, the one with the tumor making him look like Atlas. He took my hand and comforted me, uttering, "I know."

JOURNAL QUESTIONS

- *Describe a time when you felt the urge to share something personal with a stranger and didn't. What would you have said, if you could?*

- *In your opinion, are strangers just friends who don't yet know each other? Or do we carry genuine differences that keep us apart?*

- *How do you decide whether to share with someone you don't know?*

TABLE QUESTIONS

To be asked over dinner or coffee with friends and loved ones. Try listening to everyone's response before discussing:

- *Describe a time when you felt a connection to a stranger. How did you discover this? What if anything did you have in common?*

- *Tell the story of someone who you feel you've known forever; a relationship whose closeness is deeper and greater than the actual time you've known them. How do you account for this?*

A MEDITATION

- *The next time you're waiting in a public place, focus, without intruding or staring, on a stranger across the room.*
- *Breathe in slowly and absorb their presence.*
- *Breathe out slowly and let your presence flow across the room.*
- *Breathe in and imagine the life that brings them there.*
- *Breathe out and imagine what you must look like to them from where they are sitting.*
- *Close your eyes and exhale in their direction, letting the love you have today reach them like a wave.*

The Tea Master
and the Warrior

R IKIU WAS WATCHING THE CHERRY BLOSSOMS scatter on his path when he heard Taiko unstrapping his sword at the gate, and Rikiu wished the blossoms would cover his friend's sword while they tarried inside.

Without his sword Taiko looked like a huge child allowed to cry too long. Rikiu met him at the portico and even Taiko felt foolish, looking so stern, his bare feet stepping on blossoms.

As they walked the length of his garden, Rikiu wondered why they continued to meet, but knew that bugs suck at the heart of flowers and flowers love it so. The lanterns swayed, and Taiko unbuckled his suspicions on the path, and Rikiu watched them sink beneath the stones.

At the small door of Rikiu's tea room, there was a scent whose first blush could unravel selfish thoughts; a sweet bark-like scent, which could strip one steeped in calculation to a cricket hungry for a song.

Taiko knelt to shimmy through. Rikiu followed.

Inside, the walls appeared translucent and the wind through the trees shadowed them both and Taiko knew briefly that nothing was secret. The kettle began to sing, and the steam enveloped Taiko and softened his heart, and Rikiu, as he knew he would, recognized the friend he loved. In the steam, Taiko wondered yet again why he had to feel this good, if it couldn't last.

The kettle sang first like a woman dreaming of a thousand birds, then like a man swallowing his troubles, and finally like the screech of a soul fed up with earthly things. It was this final boil that Taiko longed for as Rikiu worked the leaves in the fire till they gave up their tiny stubbornness.

By the time the bowl was filled, Taiko was awash in the mood of Rikiu. Their eyes were brothered now. The steam and incense made them both deliberate as fish along the bottom. As they drank, it seemed impossible but their thoughts were close to pink.

And with Taiko's face aglow, Rikiu, his insides warming, fell to his old desire, and said for the hundredth time, "You must give it up and stay with me."

And Taiko, for the hundredth time, showed nothing. He waited, so as not to offend his strange brother, but finally, he placed the bowl to his left as he would the skull of an impotent god and bowed supremely.

As he left the steam, Taiko's heart began to harden, and, once he shimmied out the tea room, the cricket went unheard. As he passed

the lanterns swaying for him to stay, he buckled up his cold suspicions. And Rikiu, still warm inside, tried not to be sad as Taiko at the
portico swept the blossoms from his sword and strapped it to him
like another leg.

JOURNAL QUESTIONS

- *Consider the meeting between Rikiu and Taiko as a conversation between aspects of a single self. If the tea master, then,
is our inner self that finds meaning in being alive and the
warrior is our outer self that finds meaning in staying alive,
describe your tea master and your warrior, and imagine the
ongoing conversation they are having within you now.*

TABLE QUESTIONS

*To be asked over dinner or coffee with friends and loved ones.
Try listening to everyone's response before discussing:*

- *Describe which voice is stronger in you right now, your
tea master or your warrior.*

- *Tell the story of a defining experience that is founda-
tional to the tea master in you.*

- *Tell the story of a defining experience that is founda-
tional to the warrior in you.*

- *Describe your tea room and describe your sword.*

A MEDITATION

- *Boil some water for tea and listen carefully as the water sings its different voices. Note which voice of the tea you are most drawn to.*

- *As the tea steeps and cools enough to drink:*
  - *Close your eyes, take a deep breath, and let the tea master in you drink. Note what that feels like.*
  - *Close your eyes, take another deep breath, and let the warrior in you drink. Note what that feels like.*

- *As you move through your day, let your tea master and warrior talk to each other. Note where that conversation lives in you.*

From Pear to Nest

THERE WAS A NEST ALONG THE PORCH ROOF with one baby left, and the mother was in the pear tree twenty feet away, calling her to try. All the others had flown, but this one was afraid. It fluttered its tiny spray of feathers against the dry nest and cried back softly.

This went on for hours. Now the mother calling and the baby resisting seemed no different than our leap to love or our attempt to be. Soon it seemed as if both were parts of the same soul:

The more ancient calling, "You must try!"

The smaller piping, "I can't! I can't!"

The older demanding, "You were born for this!"

The smaller lamenting, "I can't! Don't force me!"

The older insisting, "All things wait on your opened wing!"

The smaller tensing, "All right! I'll try! I can't! I'll try!"

The two kept calling from pear to nest until it seemed the mother's whole purpose was to have her children fly.

Like that of a mother bird, the soul's voice perches nearby, coaxing our timid heart to spread and leap where nothing is firm.

JOURNAL QUESTIONS

- *What are you currently being called to try that you are afraid of?*
- *What is the nest you are clinging to?*
- *If the mother bird encouraging us to fly and the baby bird afraid to try are inescapable parts of who we are, describe the last time they tugged at you and what happened.*

TABLE QUESTIONS

To be asked over dinner or coffee with friends and loved ones. Try listening to everyone's response before discussing:

- *Tell the story of someone who has been like a mother bird to you; encouraging you to try, to live what you were born for.*
- *What would you say to them, if they were with you now?*

A MEDITATION

- *Sit near a tree or where you can see a tree.*

- *Wait till you see a bird in the tree.*

- *Watch how the bird takes off, flies about, and lands.*

- *During your day, reflect on how this translates to you.*

- *At night, thank the bird for its instruction.*

Waiting for the Boat

1

H E WAS WAITING FOR THE BOAT. Everyone seemed offended, most of all his father, as if dreaming something no one dreamt was an insult. Everyone thought it a crack in his character. But in his most private moments, he believed the crack led to a canyon deep within himself, and if he could only get there, the world would drop its veils.

He was waiting for the boat. His father would grumble, "And if this boat comes?" "Why then, I'll take it." "Where?" At this, he'd withdraw. His father was offended. He'd worked the land on which he was born, fought for it, extended it, only to have his willy-nilly son pout about the estate like a bird in a cage, thinking all the while, "If the boat should come, I'll take it."

There was no boat in recent memory. No dock even. Still, he'd walk among the trees at the water's edge, staring into the distance.

His mother chided the old man, "Be patient. Don't you remember how the reddest flower sent you spinning?"

His father grew angry, "There is no boat!" She drew close, "As long as he keeps dreaming, he'll stay." "Eh—He'll never be a man!" "Just leave it to me."

2

He was dreaming of the boat, dreaming of a life beyond the daily chores, beyond the family appointments, dreaming of something unpredictable. He kept wondering: *Can I use my own thoughts to power my hands?* He was unsure.

His father's only peer had four daughters. A marriage would join their lands. Within a month, they were prepared for him to marry.

He was dreaming of the boat and the seas the boat could breach, when his father took him in, proposing marriage like a deal, "Just choose whichever warms your heart and then I'll show you all you need to know."

He turned and said, "I'm waiting for the boat." His father spun him round, "I've had enough of your GODDAM BOAT! I'm giving you my life!" And for an instant he glared at his father, as if his own life were taking up space.

His mother met with him privately, "Have you ever seen this boat, I mean, in your mind?" He paced, "Why can't they just merge their little empires?"

She ran her fingers through his hair, hoping to pet and comb his mind, "It's not how things are done. You wouldn't want your father to appear undignified?"

He started to wear down. She kept petting him, "Have you ever seen this boat?" He turned and thought her genuine, "Not directly, no, but—" She pressed his lips, "Then how do you know this vessel you seek, this sense of exploration, isn't in these daughters?"

He was confused. She kissed him slowly, "Love is very much like a great unseen boat that sails across the years."

3

The first daughter was very much like his mother and try as he would to see his dream in her, she was more dock than boat. They tried for months. It was easy to lean on her. In their softer moments, he'd lay his head on her lap where she'd pet his mind. She kissed him slowly, and this held a certain safety for him, though she never allowed herself to be mussed.

She had great designs for the years ahead, and everything they did, whether reading by moonlight or swimming in the morning, each thing they did became expected and repeated; and if he should veer, her mood would weigh him down. She made love like a virtuoso, but he felt like an instrument.

When he cut it off, his parents assumed her like a daughter. The three of them applauded their similarities and thought him odd. His father secretly wanted her.

4

He couldn't bring himself to marry, for he didn't know himself. His father wouldn't speak with him. His mother played him like a harp, "I think I should have an explanation. She would have made a fine mother." He spun in consternation, "I owe you nothing. I am waiting for the boat."

Within a week, he was introduced to the second daughter, whose eyes told him she was coerced like him. They became great friends. She envied him his maleness, his ability to inherit. They'd sit cross-legged in tall grass, pretending no one could find them and she'd ask repeatedly, "Why don't you want what your father wants to give?" He could never fully answer her, till one day as the wind cuffed his face he knew, at last, "It's 'cause he's really not giving it. He's *lending* it, till he can figure out how not to die."

They laughed a great deal and wondered if they could make a life. She didn't understand his longing, but listened, for she had dreams too: of being listened to. Yes, being listened to, after all this way, seemed enough.

They met in the grass, and before long he fantasized trading places, "If I were the daughter and you the son, perhaps they'd leave us alone." She pushed it further, "What if we marry? I could run things and you could do as you please."

At first this excited them, but once they left the grass, it grew quite complicated, and he began to resent that she was content with their fathers' dream. They remained friends, and she warned him against her sisters.

5

His father cornered him, "You're running out of choices." He spit back, "No, I'm just beginning to see." The old man came very close, peering into him as a man who searches the scene for the cause of an accident, "If you don't, I'll choose *for* you."

He circled his father, "If the boat should come, I'll take it." The old man was storming out. He stopped him, "Aren't you going to ask *where*?" "No!" "But I know." "Where?" "Somewhere you can't go."

6

The third daughter was as strong as his father, but had a dream all her own. She danced in no one's shadow. She flowed into a room no matter who was presiding. He was intoxicated with her. She would not wait to be spoken to, but talked for hours, not really caring if anyone would listen.

He envied that. Next to her, his boat seemed insignificant. For now there was no defiance in it, and he was terrified she would swallow up his boat and claim it as her own.

She took him up a mountain and danced till he was sure she'd forgotten he was there. It made him feel small. He went to go, but she burst out, "No! Not Yet!" and kept inventing steps. He watched her twirl so satisfied in her own dream of things and wondered if he made his father feel this small.

He told her of the boat. She spun to a halt, "Why *Wait?*" She frightened him, "Go *Find* It!" "But I don't know where to look." She, breathing heavy, swaggered in his face, "That's what searching's all about." It made him breathe heavy. She beckoned him on. He started after. She bounded playfully. He couldn't keep up. He loved her as much as his dream. She wouldn't marry him, but vowed to go with him, should he find the boat.

7

His parents softened at his rejection. He was depressed. It was in this state that he met the fourth daughter whose eyes were pure water, whose very breath was compliant. But she had no dream at all: no dream of freedom, no dream of love, no urge to dance, no urge to control.

Within days, she attended him and filled him for she being water had found a great hole. Then like a sponge she'd soak up his unhappiness and leave him empty. He would go to her when he was in need of emptying or filling, and leave immediately, for once relieved, she seemed to vanish.

Even his parents didn't want her, and yet he felt more calm with her than when dreaming of his boat.

8

He walked among the trees at the water's edge, wondering if this all had been a dream, and if so, who were these other selves parading as mirrors before him. He stared into the distance, tired of being petted and of petting himself; tired of resisting control and controlling himself; tired of being expected and of expecting things himself; and tired of waiting.

He began to see the trees as planks and vines as rope. He began to build the hull in his mind, went for some tools, and when he returned, the third daughter was dancing over roots, offering to be his mate, if he would only build his life.

JOURNAL QUESTIONS

- *Is there something you are waiting for in your life? What pain or fear do you hope it will relieve? What emptiness or loneliness do you hope it will fill?*

- *Toward the end of the story, the son wonders if the four daughters are "other selves parading as mirrors before him." Explore what traits each daughter might represent and describe your own relationship to the trait that you find most troublesome.*

TABLE QUESTIONS

To be asked over dinner or coffee with friends and loved ones. Try listening to everyone's response before discussing:

- *Name one significant understanding of life you hold that has been misunderstood or hard to articulate. Describe your history of holding on to what it means to you.*

- *Take turns attempting an intuitive role play:*

- *As the speaker, describe one thing you are waiting for, longing for.*

  - *As the listener, imagine you are that thing longed for.*

  - *As the speaker, begin the conversation by asking, "Why are you so hard to find?"*

A MEDITATION

- *Close your eyes and breathe your way to center.*

- *Inhale and exhale until you sense no need for words.*

- *Feel the comfort of just being. Let it encompass you.*

- *Inhale and imagine that your sense of being is a boat that carries you.*

- *Exhale and feel the boat of your being drift through the current moment.*

- *Open your eyes and outstretch your hands into the day, the way you would run your hands in the water passing by.*

- *Enter the day, believing for the moment that there is nothing to wait for.*

With Great Effort

THERE WAS A HUGE STONE BETWEEN THEM. For a while, each thought the other had brought it, but it was there long before them. Neither could budge it, but together they could rock it a little.

So, with great effort, they rocked it enough to create a dark space between the stone and the earth it had packed for so many years. They could have walked away, but somehow they knew: if they did, it would always be between them. So they kept rocking and wedging, believing there would be a tipping point.

And on the third morning, the huge stone, like the heaviest of tongues, finally rolled over with a thud they could feel in their throats, its underside dark with clumps of soil and broken roots. In its unearthed cavity, worms and bugs scurried from the light. Breathing heavily, they stared at the huge unearthed thing and smiled.

Now they began to roll it enough to fit a broken bough beneath it. This, too, took enormous effort. But very slowly, they were able to lift the heavy thing between them, roll it slightly on a branch of a dead tree, and do it again. And again. And again. This work went so slow, it seemed a way of life. But in this way, they moved the unearthed thing across a field to the mouth of their garden.

It was here that they washed the thing that was between them, but which was there long before them. Here, they washed it clean of clumps of earth and insects hidden in the cracks.

Once clean, they could see the veins in the stone hidden for so long. They were really quite beautiful. So they pressed their tired palms to the veins in the stone and closed their eyes in a form of unexpected prayer.

Then, they rolled the washed unearthed thing one last time and where it landed, they began a path, and this huge thing, which no one before them could move, became the first stone. Though they seldom speak of it, those who hear the story somehow know that this is how what seems immovable becomes a foundation.

JOURNAL QUESTIONS

- *Tell the story of your own great effort—on your own or with others—and where that led you.*

- *Is there something in your life right now that is asking you to give more effort to it? Describe the situation and what giving more effort here would look like.*

TABLE QUESTIONS

To be asked over dinner or coffee with friends and loved ones. Try listening to everyone's response before discussing:

- *The story tries to illustrate "how what seems immovable becomes a foundation." What does this mean to you and how would you describe this process in your own words?*

- *Tell the story of someone who has taught you about great effort.*

A MEDITATION

- *As you breathe in and out, reflect on what it means to you to try.*

- *As you breathe slowly, let images of your own trying come and go.*

- *Slowly stand on one foot and try to be still. Reflect on the effort this takes.*

- *Stand on both feet and breathe fully. Reflect on what the aftermath of effort feels like.*

- *Sit and breathe slowly, and reflect on how attention and effort inform each other.*

To Sprout an Ear

I REMEMBER—YEARS BEFORE CUTTING MY FEET in search of a path—sitting on my immigrant grandmother's hospital bed, watching her wince as they put gauze on her bedsore heels.

I remember—years before saving my golden retriever from drowning—watching a coworker cry for his dead dog, trying to understand how he could love an animal more than a person.

I remember—years before having to start my life over—racing down a farmhouse road in the middle of the night to see my father-in-law's proud eyes jut as the barn he built thirty years before was burning to the ground.

It was only later that I felt their pain, and even more, their true joy in caring for things. I realize, step-by-step, that the earth isn't large enough for those who turn away.

Just what does it take for life to show its roots—only the breakdown of everything that parades between our hearts. If I dare to hear you, I will feel you like the sun and grow in your direction.

JOURNAL QUESTIONS

- *Often, the deepest teachings take time to reveal themselves. Tell the story and the teaching of something you experienced which didn't have meaning for you till later on.*

- *How would you describe this kind of listening to a child?*

TABLE QUESTIONS

To be asked over dinner or coffee with friends and loved ones. Try listening to everyone's response before discussing:

- *Why do you think it takes time—even years—to learn of things that matter?*

- *What does "If I dare to hear you, I will feel you like the sun and grow in your direction" mean to you?*

A MEDITATION

- *Be still and reflect on your life. Note one deep lesson that has manifested over time. It can be the one you described above. Image it in your mind.*

- *Breathe out and try to remember your innocence in that experience when it happened.*

- *Breathe in and try to feel your sense of its meaning for you now.*

- *Open your eyes and give gratitude for the thing about to happen that will release its wisdom to you in the years to come.*

Moses Has Trouble with God's Instructions

About to die, Moses wants to return to the living,
then recalls, after retrieving the Tablets the second time,
his trouble with God's instructions for how
to make the candlestick holy.

I T SEEMS ODD. THE THINGS I REMEMBER MOST are circumstances of my deep forgetting. When the Tabernacle was near
completion, I climbed the Mount for Your instructions. You were
quite specific. You even showed me how to hold, how to bless, how
to maintain. I focused on every flash of light You washed across
my brain.

But as I walked back down the mountain, as I saw the people
milling, as I heard them discuss their problems—their squabbles
of whose children were aging better, whose parents acted younger,

whose lovers were more loving in more imaginative ways—I forgot how to build.

I stopped and cleared things out, certain it would all re-enter. Nothing. Blank. Gone. I was enraged. I couldn't pull a corner of its image. The carrier was barren. I had no choice. I stomped around, kept on stalling, but finally started up again.

This time, You went more slowly. I repeated each part deeply, put every other issue of my life in the basin. I descended to the world again, repeating Your instructions to the rhythm of my descending. I made it to the marketplace where a young woman was washing clothes. The sun enlarged her bosom and splashed her arms yellow. I found her sudden and alluring. I carried on and heard her clothes slosh against the stone. Then I shut my sense and let her go to nothing. But she had rinsed all Your instructions.

Again, I was just empty. I rushed back to find her. Of course, she'd vanished. I calmed, tried not to panic, closed my eyes, began to imagine the slow descending, the deep repeating. Not a trace! Twice more, for different reasons, the same thing happened. No matter what I tried, it escaped me. I couldn't properly seize the idea, could not form a clear conception.

There are only two conclusions: The thing remembered will choose itself its channel of remembering. The light will choose the day, the heart will choose the special words or warmth with which they're said. But some things defy construction, defy being anchored in the world: the light refuses to be carried, the flame itself is brilliant when using up the stick.

JOURNAL QUESTIONS

- *What is the difference between things that remain unknowable, such as why there is suffering, and things that are deeply knowable, such as our truest sense of self?*

- *Describe one thing that is unknowable for you and one thing that is deeply knowable.*

- *Why is it hard to keep track of what we know inside?*

TABLE QUESTIONS

To be asked over dinner or coffee with friends and loved ones. Try listening to everyone's response before discussing:

- *Tell the story of a time when something insignificant or petty distracted you from something significant and essential.*

- *What caused you to remember?*

A MEDITATION

- *Before you leave the house, breathe slowly, and try to feel the truest, deepest center, just for a moment. Note what that feels like.*

- *As you move through your day, notice the times you are distracted from your center.*

- *Each time, breathe slowly, and try to return, even briefly, to your truest center. Note the rhythms of your return to center.*

The Fishermen

AT FIRST, THEY FISHED FOR FOOD. It gave them a sense of belonging to nature: casting, hooking, reeling, skinning, and cooking. Camping under the stars, they were eating nature. It was beyond words. The younger liked the struggle. The older liked the wait.

They'd meet twice a year. After a while, they sought wilder places to wait and struggle: Missoula and Argentina. In Argentina, the rivers were no kill. Everything had to be thrown back. It was strange at first: to wait so long and struggle so hard, only to camp in God's silence, hungry for the taste of what they'd caught and thrown back.

The next year, the one who liked to wait wanted to go to Mexico, to try casting a net. His friend went along. Though they said very little, they were deep friends for years.

Last winter, the one who liked to wait died. The other went to Mexico anyway. As he cast the net alone, he wondered what his friend liked so much about waiting. And as he waited, he wondered why they'd spent their lives fishing for something they couldn't see that wouldn't stay put and which they seldom ate.

JOURNAL QUESTIONS

- *Describe a time when you struggled and then threw back what you struggled with or were thrown back yourself. What did this experience teach you?*

- *Describe your relationship with waiting and how it has visited you in your life.*

TABLE QUESTIONS

To be asked over dinner or coffee with friends and loved ones. Try listening to everyone's response before discussing:

- *Talk about what it is you fish for in life. It might be wisdom, love, understanding, peace, comfort, affluence, solitude, or a sense of belonging.*

- *How's it going?*

A MEDITATION

- *Sit calmly and breathe slowly until you feel centered.*

- *Imagine you are fishing inwardly with your breath.*

- *Cast your breath deeply within the dark pool that surrounds your heart and wait.*

- *Breathe deeply and strongly and see what you hook that doesn't want to be brought to the surface. It might be a fear, a worry, an insecurity, or the sharpness of a loss or wound that hasn't yet healed.*

- *Steadily and lovingly bring it, breath by breath, to the surface.*

- *If the struggle seems too great for now, cut the line of your breath and let it swim back into the deep.*

- *If you can bring it into the light before you, surround it with your love and let it squirm till it tires or feels safe.*

- *With one last deep breath, thank it for its concern, and throw it back into your deep.*

Unbreakable

MARY LOVED THE LIGHT THIS TIME OF YEAR. It had an extra brightness, especially in the morning before everyone else was up. It was particularly bittersweet today, as her dear friend Laura had died the week before. And of all the things they shared and left at one another's home, Mary this morning found Laura's robe, because the early light she so loved had shone through her bedroom window across her bed and into her closet. She took the robe out and ran her hands up and down its sleeve. It was hard to imagine life without Laura. It wasn't long before Mary put her friend's robe on. She opened the window and stood completely in the light, and soon Mary fell into imagining the world after her own death, imagining her daughter putting on her robe the morning after she will die. But strangely, it wasn't sad. No, the sadness gave way to something deeper. Now she began to sense a cascade of women putting on each other's robes: generation after generation, each aware of the one who came before, each bowing to the world that keeps going beyond us. Each participating in the tender awareness that, though we are necessary, the world can do without us. And suddenly, each, putting on the robe of the one who came before, seemed a tether of what matters: an unbreakable lineage of how fragile and precious we are. She stood in Laura's robe in the early morning light, feeling all alone but not alone. And as far as Mary's heart could see, women throughout the ages were slipping on each other's robes. She closed her eyes and began to sway. She could almost hear the secrets of one pass to the other.

JOURNAL QUESTIONS

- *If you had to choose one trait you share with others that is unbreakable, name and describe it, and give some history of the lineage this trait represents that you are a part of.*

TABLE QUESTIONS

To be asked over dinner or coffee with friends and loved ones. Try listening to everyone's response before discussing:

- *Bring to the table one item you treasure that belonged to someone you care about, living or dead. Hold it and share its story. Then let everyone at the table hold it, too.*
- *Try to describe what this item carries for you.*

A MEDITATION

- *Silently go through the things you preserve as totems or signs of love and truth that keep you strong.*

- *In this moment, choose one that you feel is worth passing on.*

- *Sit before it and breathe slowly, honoring its presence in your life.*

- *Breathe deeply while holding it and let yourself become aware of who you might pass this on to.*

The Work of the Worm

THE STORY IS TOLD by a member of the Ojibway tribe that the Great Spirit had trouble keeping the world together, when a little worm said he could help. Knowing that the secret of life lived in everything, the Great Spirit welcomed the little worm's help. So the Great Spirit said, "Help me little worm," and the little worm slowly spun its barely seeable silk, connecting all of creation with a delicate web. The Great Spirit smiled, and Its smile cast a light across the earth, making the web of connection briefly visible. The Great Spirit marveled at the little worm's industrious gift. For the worm was not clever or brilliant, but simply devoted to being and doing what it was put here to do: to inch through the earth, spinning from its guts a fine thread that holds everything together. And so the Great Spirit said to the little worm, "You have saved us little worm, not by being great or bold, but by staying true to your own nature. I will let you live forever."

The little worm was stunned and somewhat frightened. The Great Spirit saw this, "Don't you want to live forever?" The little worm inched closer, "Oh Father, the earth is big enough to cross. I fear so many years if I can't grow." The Great Spirit smiled again at the wisdom of one of Its smallest creatures.

"Very well, little worm, I will only let you *grow* into forever. I will give you the ability to spin this precious thread that connects everything around yourself. When you can enclose yourself within that web and quiet your urge to inch and squirm away, you will emerge after a time with the thinnest of wings full of color. Then you will know the lightness of being that I know." The little worm bowed and began to search for a leaf on which to grow. And this is how the Great Spirit enabled the worm to spin a cocoon and from its quietude become a butterfly.

The story tells us that everything in Creation is connected, and that what holds it all together comes from the humble work of living on earth, spinning from our guts a fine thread that holds everything together. It tells us that the experience of eternity is possible, if we immerse ourselves firsthand in the barely seeable web of connections.

Humbly, like a little worm, it is in us to work our experience—our pain and frustration and confusion and wonder—into threads of silk. Freely, it is our choice to first connect everything with our experience; and then, to make a cocoon of those connections; and third, to enter that cocoon of experience—the way a Native American sweats in his lodge, the way a yogi holds his third eye, the way a monk maintains his vow of silence. The story tells us that if we still ourselves long enough within the web of all there is, we will eventually come to know the lightness of God's being.

JOURNAL QUESTIONS

- *Describe three significant experiences of the last year and explore how they might be connected.*

- *What are they trying to say to you about the nature of life and where you are in your journey?*

TABLE QUESTIONS

To be asked over dinner or coffee with friends and loved ones. Try listening to everyone's response before discussing:

- *Do you think there is an unseeable web of life?*

- *If yes, what leads you to sense that this is so? Name one of the unseeable threads that hold the web together.*

- *If no, what leads you to sense that this is not so? And how would you describe the way life seems put together?*

A MEDITATION

- *Reflect on how a worm turns into a butterfly in a cocoon.*

- *Breathe slowly and reflect on how innocence turns into maturity in the cocoon of experience.*

- *As you inhale, consider the cocoon you are in right now.*

- *As you exhale, consider what within you is being let go of and what within you is being given wings.*

The Life of Obstacles

*Love is the extremely difficult
realization that something other
than oneself is real.*
—Iris Murdoch

The Life of Obstacles

Pursue the obstacle...
It will set you free.

G ANESH IS THE HINDU GOD who is the provider and remover of obstacles. He is typically depicted as an elephant. Ganesh is the lord *(Isha)* of all existing beings *(Gana)*. Legend has it that when given the task to race around the universe, Ganesh did not traverse the outer surface of the earth, but simply walked *inwardly* around Shiva and Parvati, his mother and father, who are the source and center of all existence. This is the secret understanding of Ganesh. For all too often, the obstacles we experience are presented as ways to remember that *the inner walk around the source*, not the outer race, is the purpose of living. The obstacles are presented to break our trance with the race and jar us humbly back to the source, and they are often removed once our deeper sense has been restored.

It is important to realize that Ganesh is a god of *embodied* wisdom who knows the life of obstacles of which he is guardian. He is a god because he has *lived through* all the world has to offer, not because he transcends it. Often, he holds in his right hand one of his own tusks, which he broke off in a fit of anger and hurled at the moon. But the moon spit it back, and he carries that broken piece of himself as a reminder of the earthly journey no one can escape.

Often, in living through what the world has to offer, we find ourselves in our own way, stubbornly gripping our own broken tusk—stubborn in what we want, how we see things, how we approach things, and how we respond to things. And so the life of obstacles, or what we perceive as obstacles, is suddenly there to break our stare and return us to what matters. Another name for Ganesh might be God's Timing, through which we are humbled to realize, again and again, that we are not the center but of the center. These stories speak to the life of obstacles that we conjure or find in our way.

A Guide to Rock Climbing

SOMETHING MAKES ME WANT TO CLIMB THIS ROCK, the way I sometimes get the urge to step into traffic or lean over the rail, thirty stories up. Not much is said. I don't resist. I lift my arms, and he snugly knots the rope around my waist, "When I tug, push out and walk right up her back."

I watch him scale the face in perfect rhythm without a rope. He tugs, and I begin sliding my legs in and out of thin cracks, working to hook my hands on small angled juts. Jamming knees and toes, I test and reach with chafed fingers and wonder: *Will the tug burn if I slip? Will the rope cut sharp beneath a rib?*

I can't find a foothold and tremble like a cancelled suicide teetering from the top floor. "Push out—" He is distant. "Push out—" I quiver and stare at this piece of stone, which in years will be worn by the wind from Whiteface over my shoulder. I freeze. My nails go still, no feeling to the knuckle.

I see nothing but small protrusions and this hand-shaped rock leading with its atrophy to my shaking wrist. My soul has rushed to my fingertips, and to let go, to slip, would let it stream like a punctured hose. My feet scramble. I fall and cling to the mass of rock too big to hug.

I am spread, vulnerable. Fear surges electric, forcing me flatter. I scrape a few yards and then the snap, the tug, and I'm a dog shot, hauled in on a leash. I hug tight. My cheek presses the stone. It grows hot from my heaving. I am seven or eight, hit between the legs with a line drive, falling to the street flush, cheek pressed to the asphalt, hearing feet and screen doors.

But the rock face is steep, and I have just lost my soul out my scraped cheek and I am stiffly being reeled in. My palms flatten as they search the stone like fossilized braille and there, just above—the same arm's reach as before—the jut of stone I slipped from. The reach seems longer, but I stretch and stretch till I breathe like a fresco, a naked figure spread on a wall with nothing left to do but reach.

JOURNAL QUESTIONS

- *Describe a time when you were winded or knocked down— physically, emotionally, or spiritually—and the only way to proceed was to get back up and face the same person, situation, or force that had winded you or knocked you down to begin with. How did this experience affect you?*

TABLE QUESTIONS

To be asked over dinner or coffee with friends and loved ones. Try listening to everyone's response before discussing:

- *Describe a time when fear made you hold on when you needed to let go.*

- *What does it mean to consider that where we stumble and try again is our braille?*

A MEDITATION

- *Close your eyes and as you breathe, consider how connected in and out are.*

- *Slowly stand and sit several times and consider how connected up and down are.*

- *Sit calmly again and as you breathe, notice how your chest rises and falls around the same air.*

- *Open your eyes and as you breathe slowly, consider how connected success and failure are as they rise and fall around the same stream of experience.*

Ahimsikha and Angulìmāla

AHIMSIKHA WAS A VERY TALENTED and good-hearted student who had great promise. His name meant *the harmless one*. His fellow students sensed he would be a great Brahmin someday. His teacher never let Ahimsikha know, but it was clear that this precocious, gentle being was an old soul—the student of a lifetime. All the other students could plainly see how much their teacher loved the harmless one.

Close to the end of his spiritual training, Ahimsikha's fellow students, out of envy, began rumors that the young man had been meeting privately with the teacher's young wife. This was laughable, like accusing a swan of being a fox. No one took any of this seriously—at first. But when the teacher saw Ahimsikha help his young wife across a puddle, the teacher started to wonder. He dismissed this errant thought at once, so strong was his love for his special student. But during the cold season, he thought his wife more distant than usual, and so he began to darkly weave.

By spring, the teacher could not rid himself of the image of his wife and Ahimsikha enjoying a closeness he secretly wanted. The dark thought possessed him and he forgot himself. By summer, his mind was filled with dark worms. And so, to rid himself of Ahimsikha, the teacher summoned his special student to give him one more assignment.

When the harmless one entered, his teacher said, "There is one more task for you to be spiritually free." Ahimsikha bowed and waited his instruction. After a long pause, his teacher continued, "You must slay a thousand beings." Ahimsikha was stunned, "But Teacher, I cannot slay a one." "Nevertheless, you will have to slay a thousand to liberate yourself from all suffering." The gentle young soul went away confused and troubled. Every fiber of his being knew this to be wrong. Why would his venerable teacher send him on such a task? Did it hold some core teaching that, being a novice, Ahimsikha could not fathom? He so wanted to be worthy. He agonized over this horrific request. He agonized over all the years of work to this point in his training. He agonized over whether this was a test. And with great difficulty, he submitted to his teacher's demand.

The next day, Ahimsikha left with knives, swords, bows, and arrows. He first came upon an old beggar, half-asleep by the side of the road. He could barely stomach the thought, but bludgeoned him in his sleep. He rushed to kill another in order not to hesitate in all he had to do. Within weeks, he had slain several. His repulsion lessened with each slaying. Curiously, he now felt nothing: not repulsed, not satisfied, not angry or sad. There was no horror or thrill. By the second month, he had lost count and so began to take a finger bone from each person he killed. He kept them on a string. It was shortly after this that he forgot his name. He soon became known as Angulimāla, which means *garland of finger bones.*

Word spread quickly as when a plague sweeps the countryside. Beware—there is a cold-hearted student who will kill you without saying a word. In her despair, Ahimsikha's mother sought out Buddha and beseeched him to save her son. Buddha touched her forehead with his thumb and sent her home. Then, Buddha himself set out on the road where Angulimāla had been slaying travelers.

As Buddha walked slowly down the road, Angulimāla could see one more victim that would bring him closer to his thousand. Crouching like a tiger, Angulimāla waited, then jumped and started rushing behind Buddha. But the holy one did not turn or hurry. He just kept walking slowly. Angulimāla called out, "You'd better run, my stranger! These are your last moments!"

Without turning, Buddha kept his calm. Mysteriously, the more Angulimāla chased Buddha, the more he went nowhere. In fact, all his weapons grew too heavy to lift. But Angulimāla, like a large cat incensed by the taste of blood, kept trying to lift his weapons and strike the strange traveler. Finally, Angulimāla was exhausted and sweating. Buddha turned. They faced each other and Buddha, after a long silence, said, "I have stopped. You have not stopped."

Angulimāla was arrested in place. Breathing heavily, he snarled, "You say you have stopped, but you keep going. You say I have not and yet I can't move. What have you done?!" With no answer, Buddha came very close to Angulimāla's face and called him by his inborn name, "Ahimsikha, where have you gone?"

When he heard his original name, Angulìmàla dropped his string of finger bones and looked at his hands. They were swollen and bloody. He started to remember who he was and all he'd done. He fell to his knees, ashamed and disgusted. It was then that Buddha touched his forehead with his thumb and asked, "Ahimsikha, are you ready to give your life for all the harm you've done?"

And Ahimsikha—pained to awaken in this murderer's body, pained to know that he had caused so much pain—wept and answered, "Yes, yes, a thousand times yes." He told Buddha to send for the authorities, that he would be still and not resist. But Buddha circled Ahimsikha and continued, "There is always time enough to die." He then lifted the young man's chin, "Are you willing to reclaim your life by facing all the harm you've done?" Ahimsikha couldn't speak. He just nodded and wept, again and again. At this, Buddha whispered in his ear, "Then patience, Ahimsikha. Be patient and wait."

So with a swollen heart and swollen hands, Ahimsikha was broken back to the beginning. He followed Buddha and took refuge as a monk. And under Buddha's protection, the remorseful Ahimsikha discovered that he had a gift for alleviating the pain of childbirth. In time, expectant mothers were brought to him from all over the land. And just as quickly as word spread when Angulìmàla was killing everyone in his path, word spread that a healer was easing the pain of birth. More and more husbands were bringing their suffering wives to the harmless one who could ease their pain.

But Ahimsikha felt nothing: not goodness or satisfaction, not his own sadness or the relief of their pain. He could not hear the many gratitudes coming his way. Instead, he could only feel the blows he had inflicted as Angulīmāla. They followed him everywhere. This went on for a lifetime within a lifetime until Ahimsikha went to Buddha, pleading, "What should I do? I can't endure the pain. I want to die." And Buddha rocked the harmless one in his arms, whispering, "Wait. You are stopping. You must feel the thousand deaths and the thousand births and let them all empty you." Ahimsikha wept in Buddha's arms and Buddha just held him quietly till the sun went down. When Ahimsikha had no more tears, Buddha said, "When you can feel the first cry and the last cry as one and the same, then you will receive peace."

In this way, Ahimsikha had to stay alive for years, alleviating by day the pain of those giving birth and absorbing by night the wounds he had inflicted as Angulīmāla. Indeed, a thousand days and nights came and went. By now, his fellow students had grown and moved away. Some even brought their wives to him in labor without knowing it was him. By now, his teacher had grown old and died. By now, he wondered if he had ever been Ahimsikha or Angulīmāla, or some flicker of spirit waiting to enliven the two.

Years had passed but the families of those he'd slain had never forgotten the cruelty of Angulīmāla, and the families of those he'd helped into the world had never forgotten the kindness of Ahimsikha. And on the morn of the thousand and first day, he exhaled, at last, and it began to rain. It was beautifully silent, and Ahimsikha finally heard nothing. Tears began to flow from that felt place within and he could accept all he'd done to help and harm. And as his huge heart cracked without a sound, he slouched like a root and died.

JOURNAL QUESTIONS

- *Describe a time when you had forgotten who you truly are or gave yourself away. How did you rediscover yourself?*

- *In your current life, what have you not stopped? What do you need to stop that keeps murdering your energy? Enter that conversation with yourself.*

TABLE QUESTIONS

To be asked over dinner or coffee with friends and loved ones. Try listening to everyone's response before discussing:

- *Who is responsible for what happens to Ahimsikha?*

  - *Do you know someone who has both helped and done harm? How do you regard them as a person?*

  - *What is the worst thing you have done and the most helpful? How do they define who you are?*

A MEDITATION

- *As you breathe slowly, consider something harmful you've done to someone, large or small. Let yourself feel the impact of this action.*

- *As you breathe deeply, consider something helpful you've done for someone, large or small. Let yourself feel the impact of this action.*

- *As you inhale and exhale slowly and deeply, let go of both the harm and good you've done, and simply feel the nameless being under your name that is capable of both.*

The Holes of a Flute

F OR MUCH OF HER LIFE, a beautiful woman with many gifts
had tried love after love, only to be hurt several times. At last,
her enthusiasm for love had been darkened and she could only feel
her many wounds. This made her move through the days with a
great weight.

One day, toward the end of summer, she came across a sage. He
seemed to appear out of nowhere. Though he seemed equally eaten
up by life, he had a glow and a smile that she couldn't understand.
In fact, his radiance was painful as it only accentuated her inability
to glow or smile. She tried to walk away from him but somehow
circled back.

He looked up and greeted her. She said nothing. They stared at
each other, and in their stare, the sage could see how pained she was.
He said, "Why don't we sit for a while?" And the beautiful woman
with as many gifts as wounds collapsed more than sat.

They shared some bread and water. And having eaten together, the sage began, "It is a simple fact that a flute can make no music if it has no holes."

She muttered back, "Why are you talking to me about flutes?"

The sage continued, "Each being on earth is such a flute, and each of us releases our song when Spirit passes through the holes carved by our experience."

The beautiful wounded woman dropped her shoulders, "I'm tired of experience."

The sage chuckled, "Like it or not, this is one of the purposes of suffering."

She took his hand violently and placed it on her heart, "Here! Can you feel my suffering?!"

The old man's smile softened and his radiance grew brighter, "Oh, my child. You came to me for this. Let me assure you that since no two flutes have the same holes, no two flutes make the same music."

She began to tremble.

He moved closer in his radiance, "And no two beings sing the same song, for the holes in each life produce their own unrepeatable melody."

She held his ancient hand to her heart and began to cry.

He tried to console her, "You are unrepeatable."

It seemed that tears were streaming from all her wounds.

He held her face, "All of this to say, there is a great ongoing choice that awaits us each and every day: whether we go around carving holes in others because we've been so painfully carved, or whether we let Spirit play its song through our tender experience, enabling us to listen to the miraculous music coming through others."

She looked to him through her tears. She could now receive his gentleness. He simply shrugged in humility and looked skyward to the mysteries, "My child, we carve and cry when it is we who are carved in order that we may sing."

She rubbed her eyes and took a deep breath. When she looked again, he was gone.

JOURNAL QUESTIONS

- *If you were to describe yourself as an instrument, what would it be? Now imagine a myth of origin: how were you made and what has your life as an instrument been to this point in time?*

TABLE QUESTIONS

To be asked over dinner or coffee with friends and loved ones. Try listening to everyone's response before discussing:

- *Tell the story of a hole that life has carved in you, and, if possible, speak to the music or lesson that is coming through you.*

A MEDITATION

- *If you can, meditate while listening to flute music.*

- *As you listen, try to breathe in rhythm with the music.*

- *As you breathe, let the music move through you.*

- *As you breathe, feel, if you can, the music of your spirit moving through the holes carved by your experience.*

- *As the music ends, breathe into the silence and just feel the edges of how life has opened you along the way.*

The Great Awakening

HE HAD AN IMPULSE WHILE LYING to tell the truth. It felt like a flutter of heat behind his eyes, and only when he was true did the impulse return. This time, while sleeping, the impulse made him wake. And oddly, during his day, while not caring about things, the impulse seemed to say, "Not caring is sleeping and now you must wake." At this, he hesitated, afraid to care, and the impulse remained quiet until an old woman fell on the bus and he cupped her bleeding head, and after the ambulance sped away, he couldn't close his hand smeared with her blood. The whole way home he couldn't close his hand, and her blood washing down his sink seemed to say, "To care is to bleed." The next day he noticed the eyes of strangers, and at a meeting he said what he thought.

By now, he called the impulse a voice, and the voice only came when he was awake. It only appeared in the midst of sudden care. Outside a restaurant some teenagers were teasing a cripple. The voice said, "Embrace her." He shooed the boys and went on his way. In the woods, the voice appeared as the sun hit a huge elm. It said, "Climb the elm." Instead, he felt the wind through his hair. And when his wife was sleeping beside him, the voice said, "Understand her pain." He watched her all night with a finger on her hair.

By now, he looked for the voice and called it his spirit. When empty and confused, his spirit rushed behind his eyes and said, "You must never pretend." When lonely, his spirit pounded in his heart and said, "You must embrace everything." When afraid of death, his spirit moved in and out of his lungs slowly, and, appearing as his breath, it said, "You must hold on to nothing as you hold on to me." When he longed to be free, his spirit collected in his throat, and, appearing as his urge to cry, it said, "You must give up all secrets." But it seemed dangerous to have no secrets and foolish never to pretend, and every time he reached out, he was hurt and left with nothing.

He lived this way for years, and his spirit was silent. Then his wife died, and his spirit returned as a storm of grief knocking down his mind. He wanted to run, but his spirit knocked down his will to move. He wanted to die, but his spirit knocked down his will to die. He wanted to cry and his spirit opened the pores of his soul and the river he had kept locked within his whole life washed the mud of his secrets, washed the grit of his deceit, washed the silt of his pretense, and he was left with nothing.

And his spirit then whispered, "Take hold of this nothing." And he, being broken, now embraced the tree and found his spirit there. He, being filled with nothing, embraced his own death and his own death stopped chasing him. He, being free, now lingered in the moment and found his spirit always there. And drained of his fears, his spirit whispered, "I am in everything." And he laughed to think his heart was in the stranger and the tree, and he was humbled to realize that the fish opened on his plate and the cripple were inside him. And he wished with an ache that could crack a mountain that his wife could be with him. And the spirit said, "I am in everything." And he wept, for she was everywhere and nowhere and he embraced the silence, believing it was she. And the spirit said, "Go forth and be naked of all intent." And he entered the days that were left with nothing but love, nothing but love, nothing but love.

JOURNAL QUESTIONS

- *In the story, the man's spirit instructs him to stop pretending, to give up secrets, and to embrace everything. Being human, we all struggle with these. Describe where you are in your journey around pretending, having secrets, and embracing everything.*

- *From your view, what is the great awakening?*

TABLE QUESTIONS

To be asked over dinner or coffee with friends and loved ones. Try listening to everyone's response before discussing:

- *What does this story say about the nature of how we grow?*

- *At the end of the story, the spirit says, "Go forth naked of all intent" and the man lives out his days with nothing but love. Given your own experience of life, what does this mean?*

A MEDITATION

- *Close your eyes and meditate on something small that has recently called to you. It might be a bird you saw on the way to work. Or a song you heard just the beginning of as you turned your car off. Or the smile of a friend that prompted a question you didn't ask.*

- *Breathe slowly, noticing your in-breath, and consider how this small thing could be a thread that, if pulled, might open you to a greater presence of spirit and connection.*

- *Breathe deeply, noticing your out-breath, and visualize following the bird you didn't follow, or listening to the rest of the song you didn't hear, or having the conversation that might have arisen from asking your friend the question you didn't ask.*

- *Open your eyes and enter your day ready to follow the next small thing that calls to you.*

The Bridge and the Elephant

IN THE DREAM, I WAS WORKING HARD to finish a bridge to cross some river whose current was strong. It seemed important to get where I was going, though I couldn't put where I was going into words.

Just as I finished the arc of the bridge, an elephant appeared in the water. It was stepping down the middle of the stream. When it was squarely beneath my unfinished bridge, it stopped to douse itself with water. Then it stared at me.

All at once, the sheen of water on its back made me question why I was building a bridge in the first place. It made me question if what I was crossing really needed to be entered. It made me wonder: If I were to enter the stream rather than cross it, would I have a different sense of where I was going?

In the days since the dream, the image of the elephant under the unfinished bridge has made me consider obstacles differently. Now when I stumble before things I don't understand, I try to remember the elephant dousing itself in the middle of what I thought I had to cross and ask myself: Is the thing in the way something I need to cross or enter? If it's a difficulty involving love or fear, where will I be led by crossing it? Where will I be led by entering it? At each turn, I find myself needing to know: What must I face and what must I bridge? And when are facing and bridging deeply the same?

JOURNAL QUESTIONS

- *Describe something currently in your way. Consider whether it is something you need to cross or enter.*
  - *Where might crossing this obstacle lead you?*
  - *Where might entering this obstacle lead you?*

TABLE QUESTIONS

To be asked over dinner or coffee with friends and loved ones. Try listening to everyone's response before discussing:
  - *Tell the story of a bridge of some kind that you contributed to building.*
  - *How did the need for this bridge become known?*
  - *Have you crossed what the bridge was made to cross?*
  - *Is anything different in your life for this act of bridging?*

A MEDITATION

- *Sit quietly and as you breathe, allow yourself to feel your soul as a bridge that can grow over anything.*

- *As you breathe deeply, feel where the bridge in you resides, waiting to be of use.*

- *Exhale slowly.*

- *Again, sit quietly and as you breathe, allow yourself to feel your soul as an elephant that can enter anything.*

- *As you breathe deeply, feel where the elephant in you resides, waiting to be of use.*

- *Exhale slowly and enter your day with the patience to discern which you need today: the bridge or the elephant.*

Abe and Phil

Abe Greer was eighty-four. He'd lost his wife, Helen, almost ten years ago to emphysema. Reluctantly, he moved to the Bay Area to be near his children, Phil and Rachel. Rachel was the firstborn. She was a nurse at Pacifica Medical Center and Phil, well, Phil was a disappointment. Abe had wanted his son to become an architect. He thought architecture was a noble profession, a place where function and beauty met. He thought it a useful art, and it was his chief failing in life that he didn't have the aptitude to become an architect himself. But how his son became a reporter was beyond him.

When Phil graduated from San Francisco State, he returned to Brooklyn to gather some things and let his parents know he was going to stay on the west coast. He liked it there. The night before he was to leave, the chasm opened between them again. It happened around dinner. It always did. Abe was buttering his bread, "So, do you have a job?" Phil looked to his mother quickly, as if to say, "Are we

going to start this again?" Helen answered for her son, "He just graduated, Abe. Give him some time." "I'm just asking." He put his knife
down hard on his plate, "What kind of life is reporting? You watch.
Is that a way to live? Just watching?" They'd had this conversation
repeatedly. It only made Phil feel more alone and misunderstood.

So when Helen died, Rachel approached Phil, "We can't let him
stay there all by himself." "Why not?" "C'mon Phil." "Well, he can't
stay with me. We'll kill each other. You know that." Rachel had
inherited her mother's role as peacekeeper, "I know. He can stay with
me. I only ask that you help out when you can. I know he's been too
hard on you. He doesn't—" Phil didn't want to hear it, "All right. Just
don't make excuses for him. He's so self-centered that one life isn't
enough. I've always had to live up to the life he wanted. Well, I'm
done. I don't wish him any harm, but I'm done. You understand?"

Rachel had married John, a cardiologist, and they had a very sweet
boy, Kevin, who, as time would tell, had a stubborn streak that Phil
recognized as skipping through the gene pool from his father. And
so Abe lived with Rachel and John and Kevin. Abe was lucky to have
a nurse for a daughter. Since the onset of his senility, he split his time
between Rachel's home and the geriatric unit at Pacifica.

As Phil's inner tensions kept mounting, he had less and less
patience for his father's imposing nature, which was at times brutal
and unpredictable. Today, Abe was in the midst of a particularly bad
episode. Rachel called Phil to stop by the hospital. She met him outside his room, "He's been calling for you. You know what this is like."
She sighed, "Just stay back a bit and don't be surprised." They could
hear their father bellowing from his bed, "Where is Phil?! I want to

see my son!!" Phil rolled his eyes and tried to muster some resolve as Rachel gave him a kiss, "C'mon, I'll go with you."

"Where is Phil?! I want to see my son!!" Phil was amazed at how frail his father looked lying in that bed. There were a few stray hairs zigzagging from his balding head. He'd lost weight in his face, which made his eyes bug out. It made him look mad. Rachel went to one side of his bed, and Phil softly walked to the other. He leaned close and said, "Here I am, Dad." Abe stared at him blankly. Phil took both his hands and stared back, "I'm your son."

His father looked to his daughter and barked dismissively, "Who is he?! I want to see Phil!!" Though he knew his father's condition, this cut Phil deeply. To him, this outburst wasn't so much the Alzheimer's speaking, as it was the unmasking of how his father had regarded him for years. Nonetheless, Phil pushed on. He pulled an old photo from his wallet and showed Abe a picture of the two of them, confirming gently, "See, Dad, it's me—your son."

His father grabbed the photo and scrutinized their likenesses. For a second, there seemed to be a softness rising in his frazzled face. Phil tried to move into that opening, "I'm your son. See?" But Abe hardened his stare and barked, "I know that! But I want to see Phil! Where's the *Real* Phil?!" This made Rachel end the visit, "Why don't you rest now?" "I don't want to rest! I want the *Real* Phil!!" Abe was getting louder, and Rachel reluctantly buzzed another nurse, calling for a sedative.

Back in the hall, Rachel tried to console Phil, "I'm so sorry. He doesn't know what—" Phil put his hand up, "Don't. We both know he meant it." They hugged each other, and Rachel tugged her brother's sleeve as he began to turn away. "Hey, I love you." Phil gently pulled her ear, "I know."

This moment of trying to appease a crusty old man had burned to the core of Phil's sense of worthlessness. He would never stop hearing his father bark madly in public, "Where's the *Real* Phil?!" He couldn't escape it now. It frightened him and exhausted him. He just walked the streets for hours, hating his father and longing for what they never had. Finally, he met his friend Ephraim in their favorite bar. Ephraim patted the empty stool next to him, "You look terrible."

They talked it through, and while he felt some relief to be sitting there with his dearest friend, he couldn't rid himself of this growing agitation. Now he was carrying a low-level rumble of fear in his chest. Even while they talked, even while he felt understood by Ephraim, even as Ephraim confirmed the cruelty of it all, Phil was obsessed with his sitting on this stool. He had sat there hundreds of times, but now he couldn't help but wonder if this was who he was—a stool sitter. His father's bark was taking over his self-perception. He was beginning to hate himself.

When so many things start to unravel at once, it's a sign from the gods. It's more than tragedy. It's nothing less than the beginning of a rearrangement of life. This is what Ephraim had read that morning in a book about the sages of India. And here, his friend was being rearranged.

Ephraim thought to tell him all this. But he knew Phil wouldn't be able to hear it, precisely because he was experiencing it. So he simply listened and asked more questions. And listened some more. Phil talked about his mother and his sister and growing up, and the tough, relentless immigrant Abe.

Phil paused and stared at his feet while Ephraim looked at his friend, trying to imagine the picture Phil was carrying inside. Phil was tightening with anxiety. He felt a complete failure and, through the haze of the beer, he looked about the bar at all his counterparts, and, for a moment, he couldn't find the door. It made him panic, "Ephraim! Where's the door? I can't find the way out! Where's the door?"

JOURNAL QUESTIONS

- *Is there a voice that takes up too much space in your head? Whose voice is it? What does it keep saying to you about yourself and the world?*
- *Enter an imagined dialogue between your true self and this dominant voice with the intention of quieting that voice so that your own voice can be heard.*

TABLE QUESTIONS

To be asked over dinner or coffee with friends and loved ones. Try listening to everyone's response before discussing:

- *Describe a time when you were encouraged or pressured to be something you are not and how that affected you.*
- *As we all live longer and longer, the quandaries of caring for our elders become more and more pressing. Discuss the paradox of caring for someone who can no longer care for themselves and the need to live your own life.*

A MEDITATION

- *Sit before a mirror and breathe steadily with your eyes open.*

- *Allow your breath to take you to a place of surrender.*

- *Inhale slowly and imagine yourself in a long moment where you are not able to care for yourself.*

- *Exhale quietly and feel the vulnerability of such a moment and your need for the kindness of others.*

- *Close your eyes and return to yourself as you are today.*

- *Inhale quietly and open your eyes before the mirror and see your own care and strength.*

- *Allow your breath to take you to a place of resilience and compassion.*

- *Exhale slowly and feel your capacity to care for someone other than yourself in this moment.*

- *Close your eyes again and with each in-breath, feel the part of you that needs to be cared for, and with each out-breath, feel the part of you that can care for others.*

- *Open your eyes and look into the mirror; knowing that this is how we take turns in our time on earth: need and care, surrender and resilience.*

- *Allow your breath to take you to the wisdom of this endless compassion, of which you are a small part.*

In the Mirror

THE QUIET MAN FILLED WITH WORRY kept shaving while his
soul kept whispering beneath his reflection:

Loving yourself is like feeding a clear bird no one else can see.
He felt the razor pull and wondered if it was getting dull.
You must be still and offer your palmful of secrets like delicate seed.
He took a few swipes and held the razor under the faucet.
*As she eats your secrets no longer secret she glows and you lighten and
her voice which only you can hear is your voice bereft of plans.*
The steam of the water cleansed the small blade.
*And the light through her body will bathe you till you wonder why the
gems in your palm were ever fisted.*
He wasn't looking forward to the day.
Others will think you crazed to wait on something no one sees.
Taking his mind off what he was doing, he nicked his chin.
But the clear bird only wants to feed and fly and sing.

"Damn me!" he said.

She only wants light in her belly.

The small cut stung as he tore a square of toilet paper and pressed it to his chin.

And once in a great while if someone loves you enough they might see her rise from the nest beneath your fear.

JOURNAL QUESTIONS

- *Describe one thing that gets in the way of you loving yourself. Tell the story of this impediment.*

- *When the worrisome man cuts himself, he says "Damn me!" Just then his soul whispers that the clear bird within him "only wants light in her belly." Starting with these lines, imagine and journal a conversation between your "Damn me" worry and your "light in her belly" soul.*

TABLE QUESTIONS

To be asked over dinner or coffee with friends and loved ones. Try listening to everyone's response before discussing:

- *Name two things you want or aspire to and trace them back to what first led you to them.*

- *When you consider what you care about beneath all your plans, what do you learn about yourself?*

A MEDITATION

- *Sit in front of a mirror and meditate.*

- *As you breathe in and out, watch yourself as you would a nameless creature nesting in nature.*

- *As you breathe in and out, feel your true self flutter inside the nest that is you.*

- *Close your eyes and feel your true self flutter in rhythm with your heart beating.*

- *Open your eyes and feel your own presence without judgment.*

- *During the day, when you become aware of your heartbeat, feel your true self flutter inside.*

Poise

A SMALL FLOWER GROWING OUT OF A STONE quivers high above the worn paths. Its fragrance drifts down shore where a young woman is contemplating suicide, and something in the hint of flower lifts her depressed head for a moment, but the fragrance dissipates, and she sinks again, staring at the waves, wondering why. The scent is picked up by a gull, matted in its feathers. It makes the gull fly wildly through the only cloud, through the white center of nothing. An old man in a fishing boat is stunned by the swift charge of the gull into open sky. He relaxes his net, and, underneath the shadow of the boat, the tangled angelfish squirm free.

JOURNAL QUESTIONS

- *Describe a time when something in nature caused you to relax your grip.*

- *In the same way that a flower can grow out of a stone, tell the story of how something fragile and fragrant grew out of a hard place in you.*

TABLE QUESTIONS

To be asked over dinner or coffee with friends and loved ones. Try listening to everyone's response before discussing:

- *Tell the story of a time when you witnessed how interrelated all things are and how one thing impacts another.*

- *Why do you think this story is called "Poise"?*

A MEDITATION

- *Sit quietly and reflect on how connected all things are.*

- *Breathe deeply and reflect on how so much of life is happening at the same time.*

- *With each exhalation, send your love like an unseeable wave out from your center.*

- *With each exhalation, picture these waves of kindness softening all they wash over.*

• *With each breath, picture others breathing; picture all the waves of compassion relaxing the tangle of living things, though you can't see where or how.*

Wu Wei's Pot

THE KING ASKED THE MASTER POTTER to shape a pot with a strong foundation and a thin lip from which to drink. Wu Wei had made many in his time. This was a simple request. He asked to watch the King and his chancellors to see how they used such pots. So Wu Wei attended a banquet where he saw the hard use and breakage of rough living. Then he went to work.

He spun the clay on his ancient wheel. But this pot resisted being brought into the world. It would not center. Wu Wei had to hold the clay for a long time before it would yield to his hands. Once trimmed, it had to dry. The King was impatient, wanting something special to show his court. But Wu Wei said that this pot had to be wood-fired for many days to tame its shape.

The King didn't understand but left the potter to his secret ways. Not wanting to fire it alone, Wu Wei sat the stubborn pot on a shelf in his shed for months till the other potters had enough. Together, they fired the large sleeping giant that was their kiln. For one week, day and night, the fire was fed constantly, and the King's pot waited to be born in the midst of hundreds. Not special in the least.

It took a week for the fire to cool. When opened, many of the pots and urns were warped and brightly flashed. When the King's pot was handed to Wu Wei, it was still warm and the reddest markings made it seem perfect. The lip was thin as flame itself. But the bottom had a crack. Wu Wei was pleased, but tired. He went to sleep.

The next day, he brought the beautifully cracked pot to the King. At once, the King saw the unrepeatable coloring and the utter thinness of the pot's fine lip. Then he felt the crack underneath. He gave it back, "You call yourself a Master? This is not finished!" Wu Wei put it back in the King's hands, "The fire always has the last word, your Highness." The King was insulted and ordered Wu Wei to try again.

Wu Wei bowed and withdrew. On his way from court, a little boy was dumbstruck by the coloring of the pot. Falling to his knees, the little boy could see the sky through the crack in the bottom. Wu Wei helped the boy up and gave him the pot. Overjoyed, the boy ran home and hung the cracked pot from the edge of his roof. Meanwhile, Wu Wei began again.

It took several months, but the Master Potter chose another lump of clay, which also resisted being centered. And after stilling it, and shaping it, and fixing its form, after waiting for the others, after stirring the sleeping giant of the kiln once more—another pot was born. This one even more colorful than the last, its lip even thinner. But in the bottom, another huge crack. Wu Wei was doubly pleased as he let it cool.

The next day he brought the second cracked pot to the King, who was more eager than before. The King at once was stopped by its beauty. But as he held it, he quickly felt the godforsaken crack. He smashed the pot and dismissed Wu Wei.

That night, while Wu Wei dreamt of flames cracking the sky, the King dreamt of being a little boy. And as a little boy, he fell in love with cracks and the pots that reveal them. In his dream, the King was startled to see his heart as a cracked pot hung from the edge of a roof. But this cracked heart was his and not his. Somehow it belonged to everyone. And suddenly, those tired of the world were falling on their knees to drink from the rain that was dripping through the crack in the heart that belonged to everyone.

The King woke in tears and rushed to put the smashed pot back together. He couldn't and summoned Wu Wei to make him another. After several months, the Master Potter returned. This time, the King closed his eyes and searched right away for the crack in the bottom and was relieved to find it there.

From that day, the King forbid anyone to call him King and when alone, he drank from his knees, accepting a drop at a time through the crack in his heart.

JOURNAL QUESTIONS

- *Tell the story of a time when what you felt was a crack turned out to be an opening.*

TABLE QUESTIONS

To be asked over dinner or coffee with friends and loved ones. Try listening to everyone's response before discussing:

- *In the end, the King looked for how to accept the flow rather than control it. What do you think this means and how does it show up in your daily life?*

A MEDITATION

- *Sit quietly with your palms open and up.*

- *As you breathe, reflect on some aspect of yourself that you consider cracked or flawed.*

- *As you inhale, reflect on who taught you to look at yourself this way.*

- *As you exhale, let go of your inherited judgments and simply look at your own landscape freshly.*

- *As you inhale, consider how the Grand Canyon, perhaps the greatest crack on earth, is considered one of the world's most beautiful miracles.*

- *As you exhale, look again to your own crack or flaw and accept it as your own Grand Canyon.*

- *Close your eyes and vow to climb its rim and take in its view.*

Stories of the Old World

H IS GRANDFATHER WAS FULL OF STRANGE STORIES of the
old world. Whenever he'd start in, his father would sigh and
leave the room. But he loved to listen to his grandfather and would
follow him to the back of the garage where he'd find him repairing
things. This morning he watched him hammer at a broken bird-
house, then quietly asked, "What's a Shiva, Grandpa?"

The night before at dinner, his father was complaining that he
had been passed over at work; that a younger star had been given the
promotion his father had been working for. When he demanded an
explanation, his father was told that the young man was more visionary and better trained. His father was hurt and sad, but it came out
as anger. Grandpa listened, but finally said in a quiet tone, "It does
us no good to play the victim. Shiva only breaks us down to have us
form again." His father overturned his plate and stormed out.

"What's a Shiva, Grandpa?" His grandfather put his hammer
down and smiled, "Come here, you precious thing. You are a listener,

aren't you?" He brought him outside and they sat beneath the tower-
ing maple, "See this tree we're sitting under? Before I was born, it
wasn't even visible. Its tiny seed was somewhere underground, and
one day it sprouted and grew into this." He placed his grandson's
hand against the trunk, "And one day it will fall apart and go back
into the earth until another seed comes along."

The boy was transfixed by the feel of the tree. His grandfather
went on, "Do you understand?" Though he didn't, the boy nodded.
The old man continued, "In India where I was born, where our family was born, the force of the seed, and the force of the tree becoming a tree, and the force of it falling apart—each of these forces has
a name." By now, the boy was staring up into the canopy of leaves,
listening to the wind. His grandfather put his arm around him, "The
force of the seed is Brahma. The force of the tree becoming itself is
Vishnu. And the force that takes things apart is Shiva."

The boy put both hands against the tree, "Tell me another story,
Grandpa." The old man couldn't believe his blessing to have a grand-
son like this. "You want a story from the old world?" "Yes, Grandpa!
Yes!"

The old man slouched against the tree himself and fell into
remembering his wife long gone. How she would have loved this
little boy. The boy now sat between his grandfather's legs, and the
old man stroked the little boy's hair as the wind through the tree
hushed them both.

Slowly the old man began to tell the story of his life and how
it led through hardship and joy to the boy's father and to the boy
himself. The wind through the tree held them gently.

The old man had tears in his eyes, and though the little boy couldn't make sense of his grandfather's stories, he so loved the dance of his voice.

JOURNAL QUESTIONS

- *Describe which part of the cycle you are in now: the force of the seed (Brahma), the force of the tree becoming itself (Vishnu), or the force that takes things apart that they may go back to seed and grow again (Shiva).*

TABLE QUESTIONS

To be asked over dinner or coffee with friends and loved ones. Try listening to everyone's response before discussing:

- *Tell the story of someone you know who has come apart and been reformed and how it has changed them or not. What lesson does their story hold for you?*

- *Tell the story of a journey that was told to you and describe your relationship to the teller of the story.*

A MEDITATION

- *Close your eyes, breathe slowly, and imagine the oldest tree where you live.*

- *Inhale and feel the wind swaying its long limbs as it keeps reaching for the light.*

- *Exhale and imagine the seed this tree came from.*

- *Breathe slowly and imagine the part in you that is still growing.*

- *Breathe fully and feel that part in you reaching for the light.*

- *Exhale slowly and imagine the seed of spirit that you come from.*

- *Bow and kiss the earth we will all return to.*

Suffering and Loving the World

My barn having burned to the ground,
I can see more completely the moon.

—from a Japanese card found on
Phyllis Harper's dresser

The Arts of Liberation

RECENTLY, I SPOKE IN THE PHILOSOPHY DEPARTMENT at
Hope College in Holland, Michigan, on the subject: What
is Liberal Arts? After all these years, after the many ways experience has worn my tongue, I come to this with a belief in the arts
of liberation. For me, underneath all attempts at education is the
question: How do we live together in our time on earth? What does
it mean to be alive? And what are the deeper skills—the ways of
seeing, being, holding, knowing, feeling, and perceiving—that help
us through the miraculous and dangerous corridor it is to live a life
on earth?

One of the professors asked with pain and sincerity, "How do
we open the minds and hearts of young people, unsure if they can
go where they are opened?" He paused a long time, then said, "I'm
concerned about leading people into places that will undo them."
But this is the crux of it, the wonder of it, the pain of it: To be alive,

in every way, is both astonishing and full of peril. It can be abundant and collapsing. And nothing else matters but gathering the resources to make it through these paradoxical and poignant straits. We must be honest about this. Seeking what matters is an adventure that will inevitably undo us. And I believe every discipline—be it dance, botany, math, or psychology—every path of knowing has something to offer to the journey of being alive and being undone.

Several of us talked further into the night through dinner and a bottle of red wine. At last, we stumbled into the deeper notions of faith—faith that when people are invited more fully into the light, that experience makes resources available that can help us negotiate the dark. So, though the prospect of pure being—of seeing the extraordinary in the ordinary—can take your breath away, it will show you eternity. Though loving everything until your heart feels it might burst at the sight of rain can make you think you will vanish, it will cleanse you of all that is false. Though watching a mother dog lick her stillborn pup will make you cry out in silence, "I can't take anymore!"—it will steam away all pettiness. Though the passages are not always fun, there is a bedrock of calm that they can return us to.

I am more concerned with those who don't open enough. As Rilke said in one of his more strident poems, "I am alone but not alone enough to make every moment holy." This is the razor's edge between suffering and loving the world.

Just what, then, is the realm of the responsible teacher? If you squeeze a drop of iodine into a glass of water, it will color the entire glass. So let's not talk about teaching only to the mind. Whatever drops we carefully place will stir through the entire beings before us. And what are we to do with that? How are we to hold them? How near is appropriate? How far away is criminal? True education is messy, never clear, and the lessons shift and the boundaries change.

So much of what we're called to do for each other is to simply listen and tend; to hold up as a mirror the shape of what the other is thinking, and to echo back with clarity and compassion what the other is saying. The job of the noble teacher or loving friend is to guide someone so thoroughly to their own center that they, in hard-earned innocence, become the teacher.

The stories in this section speak to the journey of being alive and being undone and keeping each other company as we suffer and love the world.

The Burglar

1

AFTER A SMALL SILENCE, Ted changed the subject, "Tell me the one story I should know about Melina." Bill immediately knew which story it would be. It took a minute to shift their conversation, but he wiped the blackboard of his heart clean with one long breath and began, "Well, she doesn't like to talk about it much. So, please—" "I understand." Bill took another long breath and, as they drove closer to the hospital, he related how five years ago Melina was robbed, her home ransacked. All her belongings were trampled and broken in the haste of making off with the sellable products: her stereo, VCR, television, halogen lamps. One item in particular—a small wooden sculpture of a deer nibbling on some grass—was broken beyond repair. Her grandmother had given it to her. It was Babba's deer. Her Babba had carried it through the Holocaust. It got her through Treblinka.

Melina came home just as the thief was leaving. They looked at each other squarely for a few clear seconds before the young man ran off. After being questioned by the police and filling out all the papers, Melina went home to the rubble. She was devastated and frightened. She began to withdraw and became unusually tentative. The world had come in on her and, in the days that followed, she started to shrink inside. She started to feel hidden. It was affecting her work as a therapist.

They were now at the gate of the parking garage where everyone took a ticket to be stamped inside with the name of their loved one's malady or need: oncology, medical imaging, emergency. They found a place to park on the third level. Bill turned the car off and went on, "About three weeks later, they captured him. She had to go to the precinct to pick him out of a lineup. Once she did, they held him while she filed charges."

At this point, Bill's tone shifted to one of awe and puzzlement, "Then, as she tells it, something came over her, and she felt a need to confront this guy in order to go on, in order to reclaim her space. The detective advised against it. But you know Melina. So they finally let her speak to him with an officer in the room. The detective watched through the one-way window."

Bill looked at his watch, "Oh Jesus. C'mon. We can talk as we walk." As they crossed the glass skywalk to the hospital, Bill resumed, "Well, she sat down opposite the thief and began to look him in the eye. He was uncomfortable, but after a few minutes, he started to look back. The officer moved closer. Finally, Melina asked about his life. At first, he thought she was trying to manipulate him, but it's hard not to feel Melina's presence, and so, he began to tell his story. Turns out he wasn't some villain or maniac, but an out-of-work electrician in his thirties, with a wife and a baby. And yes, he had a drinking problem, and the rent was overdue, and their baby needed medicine. And he had a bad idea."

But Ted wasn't thinking about the electrician. He was holding the image of Melina just corridors away. Little by little, Ted was falling in love with her. He was planting each story in a small garden that he was clearing for her in his heart. As they followed the signs to oncology, Bill went on, "Then she told her story: about growing up in Chicago with her grandmother; about becoming a therapist; about her belief in needing the help of others to make it through. Finally, she spoke about his breaking in and destroying her home, and breaking the one treasure she had from Babba, who was gone.

"By now, they'd forgotten the officer. They'd forgotten they were in a police station. They'd forgotten what brought them there. The thief broke down a bit and began to tremble. Now, as Melina says, they saw each other. I can hear her telling me, 'We were no longer victim and perpetrator. We were simply two ordinary people trying to make our way.'" Bill shook his head gently, "She said he no longer looked evil, just troubled."

Stories like this opened a trust in Ted that he kept hidden. Bill kept going, "Well, damn if he didn't apologize. The detective didn't trust what was happening. Melina finally stood and said, 'I accept your apology. I hope you find your way.' With that she left, and before the detective could say anything, she calmly said, 'I've decided to drop the charges.' The detective argued, trying to convince her that people like that need to be kept off the street. He tried to tell her that people like that are good at pretending and manipulating. But Melina insisted."

Bill stopped to look at Ted, "And with that, she left. On her way home, she wondered if she'd done the right thing. She hadn't planned any of it. She just wanted to face the stranger who broke Babba's deer. And, as she said, that moment kept unfolding. She surprised herself when she dropped the charges. The detective kept him for another thirty-six hours, but had to let him go. He walked right out."

Ted had to ask, "Did she ever tell you why?" Now Bill's love for Melina was everywhere, "She said she hoped that someday someone might give her a second chance." They found themselves in the green waiting room outside the oncology wing, sitting in two large blue chairs, surrounded with tall ferns, knowing that Melina was somewhere down the hall beyond the white swinging doors.

2

It was good to see Bill. He was such a good friend. And now, as Melina waited for Ted, with her head turned to the sun, something in the smell and moisture of the morning made her close her eyes and think of the burglar years ago who had broken Babba's deer. She wished she had that wooden deer to hold onto today. Just then, she heard footsteps and knew it was Ted. This made her smile. She opened her eyes as he entered the room, "Ted! Ted! Come. Sit near me." She held his hand and closed her eyes again, for the sun was too delicious. "Have I ever told you of the time I was robbed?"

Ted found this eerie. He hesitated, feeling Bill's plea for secrecy, but decided to be honest, "Bill just told me about it." This made Melina laugh, "What an experience." Ted watched her closely and decided to ask, "Any idea what happened to him?" She opened her eyes and took a long, deep breath. "Well, he wrote me a card of thanks. I don't know how he got my address. I cringed at first, but then I thought of who he was underneath all that. So I wrote back. Part of me thought, *This isn't a good idea.* But the deeper part of me thought, *If not now, when?*"

She paused and sank below her smile, "Eventually we met for coffee. I know. It sounds crazy. But I think I did it just to see if what happened in the police station was real. There was never anything between us. It wasn't like that." Her attention was drawn to a sudden breeze that moved through the flowerbed, as if the truth of that time was a fragrance that followed her. "Anyway, we actually met for coffee for a while. Then we lost touch."

"Did you ever hear from him again?" She tipped her head, "No. But a year later, I learned that he'd been shot and killed in a robbery of a sporting goods store." She bit her lip, "Ever since, I've wondered if I did the right thing. Or did I contribute to his death?" Ted was struck by how alive this incident was for her. Melina continued, "I've been around it in my mind, but I think he was in a war with himself." Ted wanted more, "What do you mean?"

Melina sat up straighter, "Let me tell you a story. I heard it from a client around the time I learned of his death. It seems there was a Cherokee chief who wore a two-headed wolf around her neck. Yes, a female chief. Anyway, the wolves were carved out of abalone and hooked with porcupine quills. One was dark, the other light. The two wolves faced each other, mouths open at the base of her throat, teeth bared. One day, her son asked, 'Mother, what do they stand for?' After a long silence, the chief replied, 'One stands for the forces of love, and the other for the forces of fear.' After another long silence, her son asked, 'Who will win?' And the chief, without hesitation, replied, 'The one I feed.'"

Now Ted was taken by the breeze through the flowerbed, which had returned, but Melina went on, "I realize now that I helped us feed the lighter wolf. If only for a while. I also know that I didn't drop the charges for him, but for me. Had I not, I would've disappeared in the feeding of my own dark wolf." Now they both were watching the breeze through the flowers, as Melina admitted, "He wasn't alone or unusual in this inner war." She kept staring at the flowers, "No, I've come to believe that those who are cruel are simply those who are losing the war."

JOURNAL QUESTIONS

- *What kind of food does the wolf of fear want from you right now? And what kind of food does the wolf of love want? Which has your attention?*

- *What enables you to trust someone?*

TABLE QUESTIONS

To be asked over dinner or coffee with friends and loved ones. Try listening to everyone's response before discussing:

- *Tell the story of someone who gave you a second chance.*

- *Melina felt a need to confront the burglar "in order to go on, in order to reclaim her space." What does this mean to you?*

A MEDITATION

- *Close your eyes and breathe steadily till you feel calm and safe.*

- *Now exhale slowly and bring into view a situation that holds fear for you.*

- *Simply breathe and look at it, knowing you are safe.*

- *Now inhale slowly and bring into view a situation that brings you joy.*

- *Allow what brings you joy to surround what holds fear for you, the way water surrounds sand.*

- *As you inhale and exhale, allow your sense of joy and fear to merge.*

- *Note what this feels like.*

Across the Sea

A s smoke covers the Statue of Liberty, I can see my
grandmother who came here a hundred years ago, how she
struggled to learn English, how she'd mutter endearing things in
Russian when she thought we were sleeping. Last night, she came
to me in dream. We were in her small linoleum kitchen during some
other war and she wanted to dance. So I held her close and we shuffled around the small table she brought across the sea, and I told her
I loved her. She laughed and said she loved the world and I smelled
the smell of centuries on her neck.

JOURNAL QUESTIONS

- *What does it mean to love the world in daily terms?*
- *Tell the story of one person, throughout history or in your life, who you feel embodies this love in some way.*

TABLE QUESTIONS

To be asked over dinner or coffee with friends and loved ones. Try listening to everyone's response before discussing:

- *Often, in the face of great catastrophe, small moments of love and kindness give us hope. Share the story of one such moment, either from history or from your life.*

A MEDITATION

- *Choose one place of conflict where violence is present in the world today.*
- *Sit quietly and close your eyes.*
- *As you breathe in, imagine a specific city or village.*
- *As you breathe out, imagine a specific street corner or home.*
- *As you breathe in, imagine a specific being suffering.*
- *As you breathe out, send your love like water on their fire.*
- *Do this at least five times.*

The Great Russian Dancer

I T IS COLD WHERE I COME FROM. People huddle around fires and bounce. So begins the dance. When I stop, I grow cold. But more, I have these holes in my heart, as if shot before I can remember. On heavy days, they feel like arrowheads, tips broken, lodged—in here, out of sight, impossible to remove. Knifelike when I breathe. Only the hand of a woman, eyes closed, her fingers spread—only this rubbing around the holes can break the arrowhead pain. Only this and to dance—to leap, to soar. In the air—I am relieved. Touch down—the holes burn. Spin—and, for the moment, the bleeding slows. Stop—and it returns; the piercing of something so empty it pulls me to the earth. Yes, choreographers design leaps and turns and arabesques. They find sad stories and tight costumes and then we rehearse.

But can't you see—it's all to ease the press of these holes! They dress me with role after role; praise the speed of my launch, the size of my calf, the sadness on my face. It's all to Inhale—*Free!* Exhale—

Pinned! I know none of their stories, none of their steps, none of the lovely hands rubbing me to rest! Even in rehearsal, the cameras pop, and reporters wonder, why can't he stop? Why does he work so hard? But God, how can you bear it?! The holes! The weight! How can you be so still? How can you not, now, lift off the ground?

And there are times I see your eyes ease as I lift, sink as I land. We are not so different. Always rehearsing, performing, always in costume—both of us. How can you bear it?

What you call practice is just dancing alone. It is cold where I come from and the border burned in the last war. Those lost burn in me as a dark and furious human smoke. I'm caught like lightning between Heaven and thirst. How can you be so still, given all that you've seen? Where do you put it? Where do you spill? Who do you touch? God—I can't bear it!

I go from town to town where you pack the house to lift when I lift, clap when I land. Now I enter—my deerlike calf propels— *Uh—Up*—Over the fire that no one sees—*Oh*—the violence of the dead easing in my leap—*Up—Up*—Higher—Longer—I feel some relief—*Up—Higher*—You gasp—Touch down—I can't bear it— *Spin*—Like a runaway planet—*Spin—Spin*—Till the arrows bleed away—*Spin—Spin*—Could I but bleed this way forever—*Faster— Spin*—You too are on your feet—*God*—Take these holes away!

I fall to my knees. You shout and applaud. I heave and sweat. You applaud. It returns. You applaud. I grow cold. You applaud. I slouch and pant, a gifted animal in your circus.

JOURNAL QUESTIONS

- *What does this story suggest about the connection between art, suffering, and compassion?*

- *The dancer in the story says, "Always rehearsing, performing, always in costume—both of us. How can you bear it?" Describe the ways you find yourself rehearsing, performing, and in costume in your life.*

TABLE QUESTIONS

To be asked over dinner or coffee with friends and loved ones. Try listening to everyone's response before discussing:

- *We do not have to be great to suffer and to seek release from that suffering. Describe one small thing you do to help disperse the suffering you feel.*

A MEDITATION

- *Meditate on a baby's cry. Feel its necessity.*
- *Meditate on a wolf's howl. Feel its necessity.*
- *Meditate on a bird's song. Feel its necessity.*
- *Meditate on human silence. Feel its necessity.*
- *With each breath in, let them merge.*
- *With each breath out, imagine that they are all different faces of the same need.*

Hill Where the Lord Hides

IN THE SUMMER OF '41, the same summer Ted Williams hit
.406, the city of Kovno in Lithuania was being liquidated by
Germans whose fingers, sore from firing, twitched. The same summer Joe DiMaggio hit safely in fifty-six games, a notice was posted
in the Ghetto saying there was work for educated Jews.

Hundreds assembled—musicians, scholars, rabbis, elders, archi-
tects, writers, lawyers, engineers, doctors—and on August 18, while
Boston played New York in a doubleheader, the educated of Kovno
crowded the gate, waiting for work, and as Ted doubled off the right
field wall, a grey truck pulled up and a squad of expressionless Germans shot them all.

I don't know what to do with this. I don't raise it to say we
shouldn't play ball. But what do we do with this kind of cruelty. My
grandmother's sister and her husband and son died in Treblinka.
My grandmother sent them steamship tickets in 1933, and they
sent them back.

Hitting, sending, giving back, waiting for work—how do we keep alive what is alive? Does tenderness matter when a throat is cut? They say a great hitter's hands pulse in the night and that survivors hear shots forever. But how do we find, tame, release these things in ourselves? What enabled Commandant Jäger to kill so many and still dab the corner of his mouth with linen after dinner, and what made Dr. Elkes cough his heart into prayer while starving in Auschwitz?

The whole world lives in each of us. Where the Auschwitz? Where the sun? How do I breathe in a sky that has accepted it all?

JOURNAL QUESTIONS

- *Describe a time when you experienced or witnessed both kindness and cruelty at the same time. How did this impact you and your understanding of life?*

- *Throughout the ages, in the midst of our suffering, humans have always cried out, "Where is God?"*

  - *Explore your own feelings about the difference between suffering and cruelty.*

  - *Given your own experience with suffering and cruelty, what is your current answer to the question, "Where is God?"*

TABLE QUESTIONS

To be asked over dinner or coffee with friends and loved ones. Try listening to everyone's response before discussing:

- *It is a timeless imagined question, but still worth asking: What makes those like Commandant Jäger able to be so cruel? And what makes those like Dr. Elkhanan Elkes able to endure with such dignity?*

- *Is such a thing as the Holocaust forgivable?*

A MEDITATION

- *Sit quietly and realize that right now, as you breathe, something tender and loving is happening and, at the same time, something cruel is happening.*

- *As you breathe, simply withstand the tension of these opposites. Do not try to make sense of them, just receive them.*

- *As you breathe in, show the cruelty you are seeing to the part of you that is capable of harm.*

- *As you breathe out, show the kindness you are seeing to the part of you that is capable of care.*

- *As you breathe in, let the kindness within and without dilute the cruelty within and without.*

- *As you breathe fully, let the kindness and cruelty of the world swirl through you into the ocean of Spirit that holds us all.*

The Painter Is Painted
(for Don)

H E WAS IN THE PARK trying to catch the colors. His easel wasn't quite firm. He was about to spread its legs a bit in the grass when he sensed someone coming from the fountain. The park was full of those who had nowhere to go. He thought, *I just want to watch the light.* The man kept coming. The painter moved closer to his canvas, poking his yellow brush intensely. He was skilled at look- ing busy. But the morning light was so disarming. It stopped him in midstroke. No dab of yellow could capture this. It was then, between strokes, that the scruffy drifter sat in the grass; right in the patch of light he was painting.

The artist kept watching the light, which now crowned the home- less man's back. The drifter was so dark, he was attracting the light to him. It was impossible to concentrate. It wasn't fair. The morning would be wasted. It was then the dark one started talking to the painter who was trying to be polite. As he rambled, the painter was struck by the light filtering through his knotted hair and wondered if having no one let the ideas just grow out of your head. So he began to listen. The man with ideas growing out of his head asked the artist, "Why do you paint?" The artist replied, "It's all about the light." The man without a name offered freely, "Then you want to come back earlier and stand behind that oak about ten minutes after sunrise."

The painter was now unsure what to paint. He stood there, his yellow brush in hand, listening to his new friend who needed to be heard, who needed to hear himself, who wasn't so different after all. The painter dropped his shoulders and sat in the grass next to him. The day grew warmer and more people happened by. The man with ideas growing out of his head started to have feelings grow out of his mouth. He spoke of lovers and friends, never citing names, and travels to the East, and making and losing money, and being lost for so long that he let go of coming and going.

The light became unusually bright, and the painter stood to cover his paints. When he turned, his new friend was gone. Like a bird suddenly gone once fed.

JOURNAL QUESTIONS

- *Describe a time when you were so intent on looking for one thing that you missed what was before you.*

- *Describe a time when you received wisdom from an unlikely source.*

TABLE QUESTIONS

To be asked over dinner or coffee with friends and loved ones. Try listening to everyone's response before discussing:

- *What does the title "The Painter is Painted" mean to you?*

- *The scruffy drifter confesses to "being lost for so long that he let go of coming and going."*

  - *Role play a conversation around this.*

  - *Have one of you start the conversation by citing the drifter's thought.*

  - *Have the other ask, "What do you mean?"*

  - *If others are present, have them be silent witnesses.*

  - *See where the dialogue goes and discuss what happens.*

A MEDITATION

- *During the day, maybe at lunch or for a break, sit in a public space quietly.*

- *Meditate for ten minutes in the open with your eyes open.*

- *As you breathe slowly, consider how wildlife in the forest is seldom seen when going for a walk.*

- *As you breathe deeply, consider how the sources of wisdom in the world are just as present and just as hidden.*

- *With each out-breath, become a safe place for wisdom to show itself, the way small creatures come out of the woods looking for food.*

- *With each in-breath, realize that when we are quiet, sources of wisdom appear and give what they know away.*

- *Close down your preferences, and let the sources of wisdom find you and feed you.*

Two Monks Climb
a Mountain

I T WAS AMAZING HOW MANY PEOPLE were coming to his talks.
Many were curious. Many were lost. Many wanted to see him
trip. Many were ready to be offended. The tall grasses where people
gathered had been trampled and matted from the many crowds, and
there was something holy about the blue emptiness of the sky. It was
midmorning when Rammohun appeared.

The crowd buzzed and bowed as he walked by. Once he reached
a slightly elevated patch of ground, the crowd grew quiet and Rammohun began, "Let me tell you a story. There are two monks. Both
have followed the Buddha's teachings all their lives. They are considered to be holy men who have prepared many years for a sacred
journey. And one day they begin. Together, they start to climb a holy
mountain. For they believe that the Buddha himself waits at the top.
But halfway up, one of the monks breaks his leg and can't go on."

Now half the crowd identified with the broken monk and half with his friend.

Rammohun allowed the notion to sink in, then went on, "Well, they stay the night, hoping to continue in the morning, but the broken monk now has a fever. It's clear he can't go on, and, indeed, he can't stay there either. He needs to be brought back into the world so he can heal. Just what should the other monk do? Should he leave his brother so he can achieve nirvana? Or carry his brother back into samsara? Tell me, what would you do? Tell me!"

A young man full of devotion blurted out, "I would make him as comfortable as I could and keep my destiny with Buddha." Rammohun spoke to him directly, "And what if you were left behind?" The young man was proud of his clarity, "I would accept my failings and get out of the way." The prophet looked at the young, devoted man for a long time and finally sighed, "And who among you will travel with this holy man?" The entire crowd laughed.

He pointed the young man out to the crowd and said kindly, but sternly, "If you were broken on the mountain, it would be your good fortune to have traveled with me. For I would forsake any goal to preserve life. But if I were broken on the mountain, it would be my great misfortune to have traveled with you." He stared at the young man with an air of disapproval, then spoke to the larger crowd, "Now you can make the mountain what you will—whatever you desire, whatever you aspire to be or have. But is any goal worth a single life? Even meeting Buddha? And what if you are meant to discover that caring for another is the summit?"

The crowd went silent and Rammohun brought his insight into

the open, "You see, all beings can be understood in this way. There are those who would leave their brothers broken on the mountain, and those who would forego the mountain of their dreams to preserve life." He kept penetrating through the opening he felt in the crowd, "The history of this kind of suffering is vast. For each era has its share of those broken along the way. When most are left behind, we have an era of cruelty. When most are cared for, we have an era of compassion. It's as simple as this: Which are you? And what will you teach your children?"

Embarrassed and offended, the young, devoted man stormed his way out of the crowd. At this, Rammohun barked, "I can't tell if he's racing up his mountain or going back for who he left behind!" The entire crowd laughed its nervous laugh, for everyone wanted to see themselves as the monk who would forego his dreams, but many realized that they were, in fact, the other who would climb the mountain at all cost. Sensing this, Rammohun declared the talk complete, "I see you've plainly landed in the middle of it. I think we're done."

JOURNAL QUESTIONS

- *Describe a time when you struggled between your commitment to where you felt called to go and your commitment to others.*

TABLE QUESTIONS

*To be asked over dinner or coffee with friends and loved ones.
Try listening to everyone's response before discussing:*

- *Tell the story of someone who climbed their mountain at all cost.*

- *Tell the story of someone who put everything aside to help those along the way.*

- *Is a balance between these two devotions possible?*

A MEDITATION

- *This is a walking meditation.*

- *As you move through your day, notice those you pass: the elderly sitting on benches, the homeless we all walk by, even your colleagues at work.*

- *As you pass them, consider in what ways, seen and unseen, others are broken on their way up the mountain.*

- *As you pause and breathe slowly, consider in what ways you are broken.*

- *As you inhale and look around, ask yourself, where is everyone going?*

- *As you exhale, ask yourself, where am I going?*

- *Open your heart and wonder, in what ways can we help each other?*

Suffering and
Loving the World

U NDER ALL OUR DIFFERENCES, we are each other: capable of anything and everything, both wondrous and horrific. Every day, in countless ways, we face the challenge, again and again, to suffer and love the world. A heartrending incidence of this erupted recently like an aneurism in the body of our society. I'm referring to the shootings in Virginia, which have stayed with me. I'm sure you heard about it. It was a televised tragedy.

Let me begin with the terrible facts. On Monday, April 16, 2007, at 7:00 AM, Seung-Hui Cho—a senior at Virginia Tech, wearing black gloves and armed with a small-bore .22 Walther semiautomatic handgun and a 9mm semiautomatic Glock handgun—shot and killed a young woman and a young man in West Ambler Johnston Hall. He left the scene and mailed a package of writings and video recordings to *NBC News*. The package was postmarked 9:01 AM.

Around 9:30 AM, Cho entered Norris Hall, chained the three main entrance doors, went to the second floor, and began shooting students and faculty.

In nine minutes, Cho fired about 170 bullets, killing thirty more innocents, and then put a bullet in his own temple. During those nine minutes, Cho had come to room 204, where Professor Liviu Librescu was holding his class in solid mechanics. A Holocaust survivor, Professor Librescu must have found the sudden appearance of cruelty and shooting much too familiar. As his students escaped through the window, Liviu held the door shut, keeping Cho out. Then Cho shot through the door, hitting the Professor five times. Cho moved on and Liviu Librescu died.

I am compelled to imagine their meeting through that door. They'd come a long way, the spirit wearing Cho and the spirit wearing Liviu, as they have throughout history, through many lives, across many cultures. This time, to meet in Blacksburg, Virginia, on a spring morning when all seemed right with the world. This time, one was Korean, lost in America, while the other was Romanian, a Jew spit out from the Holocaust.

They would face each other that morning as one more incarnation of the twin faces we each carry. This time as Cho, the loner broken by isolation, and as Liviu, the resilient one broken open by suffering. The one in so much pain that he couldn't keep from breaking everything around him, the other stripped of all pretense till he couldn't keep from embracing everything in pain.

They didn't know they would meet again that morning. They didn't know they would re-enact the battle over life we all seek and fear. They were strangers, at least in this time and place, and they were also inevitable counterparts spinning like electrons of spirit, destined to collide in a timeless paradox the rest of us keep trying to make sense of.

No one will know what either woke with that day. Seung-Hui Cho, so divorced from life that he sought the flow of blood. And Liviu Librescu, so far from the horror that changed him, that he could only think of birds and his students' names. They both dressed and shut the door behind them that morning. The one as Cho moving like a ghost desperate to crack the grayness surrounding him, the other as Liviu so cracked by his suffering that he could barely stand the wonder of another day.

Like the eye of a storm, their impending moment at the center of this tragedy was almost missed in the awful devastation of so many. But let's go back, before Cho bought his guns. Before any who were killed that day were born. Before Liviu was put in a concentration camp. Let's go back a few thousand years. There, before they were Cho and Liviu, these warring spirits met as Angulimāla and Buddha in the sixth century BC. The one breaking everything was Angulimāla. He was at large, killing many. And the one embracing everything was Buddha. They met along the road. There were no cameras or replays. But it is said that they stood before each other in silence for a very long time, when Buddha said simply, "I have stopped. You have not stopped." And legend has it that Angulimāla was undone, alive for the first time.

Will we stop? Will we ever stop? The world has always hung in the balance by a thread of compassion. As they drove to campus that morning, I imagine that Cho was oppressed by the feeling that he could not stop. And that Liviu, for all he'd suffered, was forced to stop, to put everything life-draining down. That morning, the one appearing as Cho was counting his bullets, while the one appearing as Liviu was stopped by a dogwood along the way.

But let's go back, before they were Cho and Liviu, to sixteenth-century Japan where they met again. This time, the one desperate as a ghost was a hardened Samurai. And the one who could barely stand the wonder of another day was a clear-eyed monk. There, the Samurai sought the meaning of life and was told that the quiet monk knew. So the hardened one found the monk in prayer, drew his sword, and demanded the secret. The monk kept on praying, which angered the Samurai who finally said, "Don't you know that I can kill you in a second without blinking an eye?" To this, the clear-eyed monk, without breaking his pose, replied, "And don't you know that I can be killed in a second without blinking an eye?" This time, the hardened one dropped his sword and withdrew.

But in our time, in Blacksburg, Virginia, as the dogwood was opening, the one who could not stop was shooting his way through Norris Hall without blinking an eye. And hearing the shots, the clear-eyed one did not break his pose, but recognized the shots as those sprayed in the camps. This time, the quiet one who could be killed without blinking recognized that the wheel had come around again. He told his students to go through the window as he walked toward the door. For a moment, as he turned, he couldn't tell if those scurrying out the window were his students or his fellow inmates in the camp. As he faced the door, he wasn't sure who was on the other side: a thief, a madman, or an S.S. officer.

He might have closed his eyes as he waited. Did it matter who had lost their tether to life? Did it matter if it was 2,500 years ago or sixty-three? Did it matter if it was a stone or a sword or a machine gun? Would it matter what either would say? The shots came closer and before their moment, the clear one took a long, slow breath.

They were coming close. They would meet again. But let's go back, just one more time, to Aboriginal Taiwan in the 1700s, where the spirits wearing Cho and Liviu appeared as a chief and a diplomat. This time, the hardened warrior would behead one tribe member a year. It was seen as religious. And the one tired of killing would plead and plead for the beheading to stop. And the hardened one would listen respectfully, then excuse himself and behead the one chosen. This went on for years. And finally, while pleading as another innocent trembled, the one broken open enough to stop watching, faced the chief and said, "No. This time, if you kill, it will be me." And in that small village, with no one watching, the chief, having grown to love the one worn to wonder, couldn't kill him, and the custom of beheading stopped.

Now they were again in each other's way, as so many times before. But there wasn't enough time for Cho to fall in love with Liviu. I imagine they sensed each other on the other side of that door. And without a word, Liviu's presence was saying, "I have stopped. You have not stopped." And Cho paused for a second, alone in the hall, blinded by all that remained asleep in him, pained by it.

They, no doubt, said nothing through the door. I imagine that Liviu rode his lineage in that moment. I imagine he did not blink. It was then that Cho, unable to stop, unable to feel, must have held his gun to the door and fired. And in that instant pried open, in that choice point of soul relived forever on earth, we are them. Like it or not, we pulled the trigger and we faced the gun. Like it or not, we live on both sides of the door. And what will we do next time? Will we stop? Will we break everything we touch or break open? Will we keep running from life and kill? Or face death and live?

Their moment had come. The one called Liviu stayed and faced the one called Cho yet again, saying without saying, "This time, if you kill, it will be me." It was a simple morning in spring in Blacksburg, Virginia, where the struggle that lives in each of us appeared again. And there, the still point of the Universe was wrestled briefly into view. It would be unbearable but for Liviu Librescu's spirit rising from his body—already en route to another about to be born—as Cho reloaded and kept chasing his pain down the hall.

JOURNAL QUESTIONS
_____

- *Describe a time when you were broken and what that did to your sense of life and the world.*

- *Describe a time when you were broken open and what that did to your sense of life and the world.*

- *Where do these two possibilities live in you now?*

TABLE QUESTIONS

To be asked over dinner or coffee with friends and loved ones. Try listening to everyone's response before discussing:

- *The story concludes that "Like it or not, we pulled the trigger and we faced the gun. Like it or not, we live on both sides of the door." What does this mean to you? What is your view of this?*

- *On the one hand, Cho was an individual, responsible for his own actions. On the other hand, his aberrance was produced by our society, the way a highly pressurized bloodstream can weaken the wall of a blood vessel, causing an aneurysm. Imagine and discuss what factors may have created the destructive force that was Cho.*

A MEDITATION

- *Close your eyes and reflect on the soul of Cho and the soul of Liviu.*

- *As you breathe slowly, reflect on the timeless spirit that appeared this time as Cho and the timeless spirit that appeared this time as Liviu.*

- *As you breathe deeply, reflect on the fleck of isolation that lives in you that could, if fed, become destructive.*

- *As you breathe slowly, reflect on the fleck of vulnerability that lives in you that could, if fed, become life-giving.*

- *Be aware of both your isolation and your vulnerability as you move through your day.*

- *Be careful what you water.*

Pierrot in the
Dead City

1

THE MASTER BELIEVED IN ALL HIS STUDENTS; that was what made him a master. Pierrot believed in himself and the dance. When himself, he was a match. When the dance, he was aflame.

The master said one day, "I have written a solo for you." Pierrot puffed up, "Of all the students, just for me?" The master chided him, "No. Not *just* for you. Just *for* you."

Before Pierrot could understand the master was up, "I will show you once. Very slowly. It is the dance of a clown through the streets of a city where the families are broken, their treasures stolen. Even the children seem eighty. I will show you once."

Pierrot watched each bend of foot, each drop of arm, counted the master's steps, caught the pattern at once, imagined its reversal at once, imagined three variations at once.

The master stopped, his being heavy with the burdens of that city. He seemed exhausted and changed, like a man who climbs a mountain to find his lover, a sad man who returns with nothing but the echo of her cry.

Pierrot did not see this. He only saw the steps and wanted to try them while his impression was fresh. He mirrored the master exactly, adding a flourish all his own.

The master looked through Pierrot who was breathing heavily, anxious for his teacher's praise.

"I forbid you to dance this in public."

"But why?"

"Your heart cannot do the steps."

"I don't understand—"

"Exactly."

And the master walked away.

Pierrot's pride kept him from the master for several days. But finally, at dawn, after watching the master pray by early light, he stopped him on his path, "Teach me the steps of the heart."

The master sighed, "My son, I can't."

Pierrot grew indignant, "You call yourself a master."

The master chuckled, "It is you who call me master."

Pierrot followed him, "You must tell me *something*. Here— watch—I have practiced." And Pierrot again mirrored the master's dance, even more deftly than he was shown.

The master purposely peaked the silence. Pierrot became transparent as handblown glass. The master uttered slowly, "I forbid you to dance this . . . in public."

Pierrot shattered before him, "What would you have me do?"

The master lifted his chin, "To practice with the body is not to practice with the heart."

Pierrot pulled away, "Teach me! You are a teacher!"

The master circled him as a doctor would a patient with an unknown disease, "I will not tell you what you should be. You will lose your freedom." He kept circling Pierrot, "And I will not tell you what you are not. For you'll resent all instruction." Then he faced the young man, "I will simply tell you what you are." Pierrot waited painfully. The master said, "You are too much yourself."

2

Weeks went by during which Pierrot watched clowns act like children and children like clowns. He noted the lightness in their step, how clowns danced with their eyes, how children lunged for the space out of reach. He saw a little girl chase a butterfly, unaware of her own grace, saw a cat chase a bird, saw the breezy wind dash a piece of bamboo about the day, saw the natural rhythm in everything.

At first, he wanted to jump like the girl, to pounce like the cat, to lift everything about him like sudden wind. It was then he noticed the ferryman's daughter laughing at him from a distance. But when he tried to talk, she fled, and chasing, he felt initially alive with the chase. But the longer it went on, the emptier he felt in his endless motion. She vanished and he, panting, wanted more than anything to kiss the butterfly, to talk like the bird, to unravel like bamboo, and to sit with the sudden daughter, feeling the laughter in her eyes.

When Pierrot danced for the master, the steps were barely seeable, his breathing wild, his arms obeying a motion spinning behind his eyes. The master seemed pleased. Pierrot stopped, dizzy and puffing. The master cupped his face, "You have found the source of joy. You are also out of control. You are too much the clown."

3

Pierrot was gone for months, unsure what to do. He went to many cities, though he hated cities, talked with no one, watched everyone, grew hungry, grew irritable, forgot his hunger, forgot his preferences, saw how the homeless had no need to wash, how the loveless had no need to touch, how the wealthy had no need to see, saw how thieves, like wolves, could strip a carcass in an alley, and he squat near what was left through the night and next day, watching the open eyes never move, watching the cold wind lift and drop the dead man's cuff. He squat there till his knees hurt from not moving, till stray dogs sniffed at him as well. And Pierrot began to weep, began to see all dance as trivial, began to ask without words if the hardened corpse was not happier. He wept at the cruelty of life upon its living, which he had never known. An ant crawled across the dead man's face. Soon others appeared, and Pierrot rose and walked away, leaving his innocence squatting forever in that alley.

When he danced for the master he shuffled, his head always down, not caring for the steps of the heart or the opinion of his teacher. He collapsed more than finished, and the master lifted him in his arms, rocking him gently, "My son, my son, you are too much the dead."

4

Pierrot moped about the master, never sure what to say. Finally, as he slept, the master whispered to his spirit, which never slept, "You are still pretending." Pierrot appeared restless. The master continued, "You must undo the purpose of a clown, the purpose of the dead . . ."

Pierrot woke as the master concluded, "You must let go . . ."

Pierrot sat up, "What is there to find?"

The master hushed him, "You must find—"

Pierrot interrupted, "I have no purpose."

The master sighed.

5

Pierrot was deeply troubled, and though he moped about, kicking stones and peeling twigs, parading in silence, the master knew he was still practicing. And his practice brought him to the river where he saw the ferryman's daughter, as troubled as he. He knelt beside her and saw her father bobbing in the reeds.

She began to wail, and having outgrown his master's instructions, his heart began to burst, and it brought him to his feet, and he began to circle the young woman crippled by her grief, and he began to dance with the eyes of a butterfly and the eyes of the dead.

He circled her grief with his, drew a clear turban of air about her face, and sighed with the weight of centuries, and that sigh, which he had longed for, lifted her head like a broken stalk of bamboo gently, gently until she could mend.

JOURNAL QUESTIONS

- *Tell the story of a teacher, parent, elder, or friend who, in some way, led you to your true self.*

- *Describe where you are in your journey of discovering and integrating who you are with your understanding of joy and suffering.*

TABLE QUESTIONS

To be asked over dinner or coffee with friends and loved ones. Try listening to everyone's response before discussing:

- *Tell the story of a time when you were too much yourself, too much the clown, or too much the dead, and what awoke you from this trance.*

- *Given Pierrot's journey, what is the purpose of dance, more largely art, and what can it give to the living?*

A MEDITATION

- *Sit quietly until you can feel, through your breath, a steady sense of your being.*

- *As you breathe steadily, enliven a recent moment of joy that you experienced or witnessed.*

- *As you breathe deeply, enliven a recent moment of suffering that you experienced or witnessed.*

- *Breathe deeply, allowing these two impressions to merge within you, without denying the fullness of either.*

- *Breathe fully and let your being, the seat of your true self, be a container for both joy and suffering.*

- *Allow the feelings that arise to enter your body.*

- *And whether it's a small gesture, the dropping open of your hand, or whether you are moved to your feet, in order to open your arms and spin, allow your being to express the beginning of a dance.*

The Wolf of Gubbio

1

I T SEEMED AN ISOLATED INCIDENT. Everyone felt badly for Antonio. He found three of his sheep gutted. One was still alive with whole pieces missing. He had to smother it. But the attacks recurred, though they seemed confined to the outskirts and only at night. Merchants took it as an affirmation. They were right to give up farming.

Things were safer in cluster. Wherever men could huddle, barter, or socialize seemed off-limits to the wild. Then in spring, on a pleasant day in which the hyacinth began to find their color, on a cobbled street near the heart of Gubbio, as Bertollo was setting up his cobbler's bench, as his children were kicking a woodblock in the alley, the wolf appeared prancing almost silently, the sun slick off its paws. The children didn't know it was a wolf. They thought it a large dog. Bertollo was seated at his bench hammering a broken heel when he felt an animal warmth. The wolf was very close to his thigh, breathing in his crotch. Bertollo overturned his bench and scuttled backwards like a crab. His little girl started for his side. He yelled, "No! Run! Run!" But she didn't and the wolf began to circle her. Bertollo started throwing shoes and the wolf dodged them easily and vanished down the alley.

After that, no one felt safe. There was a squint in everyone's walk. Women washed their clothes in groups by the river, with one or two husbands guarding the shore. Even the inner courtyards of the wealthy had favorite chickens slaughtered and egg baskets ravaged. The mayor's pig was attacked. It seemed less fierce.

2

There was a town meeting. The fear had made some men bold. It made others so angry they appeared wolflike themselves. They agreed to hunt the beast. Francis was at this meeting, but he said nothing. He simply watched the city's emotion coalesce into a growl. And without much of a plan, the mayor led a pack of husbands and firstborn sons to the woods beyond Gubbio where they would try to kill this wild and hungry thing.

They went at night carrying torches and knives. And while its mate's howl rimmed the darkness, the wolf pranced through the village and found Bertollo's little girl, who wasn't sure what all the fuss was about.

She saw the wolf in the alley behind their small house and slipped out to meet it. It took quite some time for her eyes to adjust. As they did, the wolf's eyes began to glow, and she could hear it panting as it came closer. She thought its eyes huge and unfocused, but they had a reddish tint that she had seen in the fires her father let burn for days.

They stood before each other for a long time. When she went to pet the wolf, it bounded out of reach and playfully pawed her. It ripped her little dress. She ran into the house and the wolf prowled the empty village, killing two cats and dragging them to the river.

By morning, the men of Gubbio had returned, agitated by a night of howling, only to find cat bones by the river. And Bertollo's little girl, afraid she'd be punished for leaving the house, was forced to say the wolf came inside and ripped her dress.

Now even their interiors weren't safe. Some of the women badgered their husbands, "Go find that crazy hoot, the one who walks the woods in rags." "The one birds speak to." "Francis, that's the one." "Yes—get Francis to talk to the wolf."

The men most afraid thought seeking out Francis was a form of surrender. But the others quietly agreed. Lorenzo said, "Why not? We could use him as bait."

3

Five days passed, and things were quiet. Maybe the wolf had moved on. People were beginning to relax. Men began to daydream. Kids began to play. But in the middle of the afternoon, there was a sudden scuffle, growling and squealing at a desperate pitch. By the time the men on guard arrived, the Mayor's pig was dead, his courtyard splattered, his fence broken, his garden dug up, his stone bench tipped.

4

Everyone was intent on killing the beast, if they could only find it. The mayor himself took Bertollo and three others and went into the woods to find Francis. After two days, they found him in a large ring of brush, a fire in the middle, birds everywhere, a fox curled near the fire, and a small doe nibbling berries from a tree.

The mayor spoke first, "Are you Francis?" Francis moved toward him and the birds fluttered to the safety of the trees, "Do you see how all the wings move away from you?"

The mayor ignored this, "We need your help." One bird returned to Francis. He held it in his palm, "It's all a matter of trust. You want so badly to fly; they sense your heaviness and envy."

The mayor was losing patience: "This wolf has been killing in our streets. No one is safe." Francis shooed the bird back to the tree: "Anything domesticated is easy prey." The mayor pressed him: "Can you do anything?" Francis stoked the fire: "I won't kill him, if that's what you want."

Bertollo erupted, "He almost killed my daughter! Is an animal more important than a person?!" Francis moved closer and spoke in a whisper, "An animal *is* a person without a conscious spirit."

No one understood him.

The mayor remained focused, "Can you convince him to leave us alone?"

Bertollo was disgusted. Even the mayor felt embarrassed to be making such a request.

Francis motioned to the world beyond his brushlike nest, "We are the guests. This wolf wants something—"

Bertollo burst in, "It's a beast! A hungry, unthinking beast—"

The mayor hushed him, "We would be grateful for anything you might do . . . We are tired of living in fear."

Francis liked the mayor and saw his animal-spirit as a bear. He looked at Bertollo and saw his animal-spirit as a ferret. He petted the fox at his feet and said, "I will try."

Francis watched them leave and knew they would try to use him to find the wolf. So he broke camp and headed into the mountains due west of Gubbio, leading them over steep climbs to the base of the other side, bringing them near a river thickly covered by undergrowth. Once there, it was easy to lose them, and since there were mountains on all sides, it would take days for them to find their way back. He left them in a valley lush with spring and started for the woods north of Gubbio where the wolf lived.

5

As he walked the depths of country he so loved, he felt himself marching to the interior where life-forms never evolve very far from their basic nature. This is why he was so drawn to animals. He felt certain they were incapable of wedging things like morality and conscience between their way and their basic energy centers.

As he walked deeper through the interior, he felt the silence grow instructive, as if words were a curtain for those unable to face truth. He was at the edge of the forest that had no paths when he saw a strange bird he'd never known. Its beak was small and always open. Its breast was blue, but its wings were a faded shade of gold. Animals are blessed, he thought, with an incorruptible capacity to evolve wholly around their one pure impulse.

This is why he loved birds. Everything, he thought, from their darting pealike eyes to the orchestration of their feathers to the lightness of their legs, is shaped by their irrepressible urge to fly. Everything about their existence is designed to make that impulse a reality. It is the same with fish. No limbs, no impediments to the urge to go below.

Even the wolf astounded him as a complete manifestation of pure hunger. Its abilities to seize, tear, and devour—developed to satisfy and nothing else. And its unnerving howl—nothing could ever rip through comfort like that empty voice of hunger.

He stopped to feel the richness of a forest with no known path and listened to the mix of animal-spirits there but unseen, each calling with a cry unique to its basic impulse. He wanted to earn his own. He felt God was speaking through the cries of animals in a precensored form, in an elemental language that man in the development of his mind was cutting off. He felt certain that each of those cries was living within his soul, though he had lost the gift of hearing them.

He was convinced that being human was the most complex gift of all: a puzzle of breath, of how to free our animal-spirit in order to expand our being. To want like a bird. Dream like a tree. Think like a wolf. Endure like a stone. To allow the variety of God's impulses their true nature as they funnel through the human heart.

6

He had walked so far into the interior that he had no sense of the outer world. He felt no sense of civilization pulling him back. He felt no need of protection, for God was everywhere: in the fallen trees he was walking over, in the thatches of light spraying through the canopy of living brush, in the stream he heard trickling with new life to his left. He approached the east side of the farthest mountain and there in a clearing at the mouth of a small cave, the wolf and its counterpart and their three wolf-cubs.

The cubs were playing like Bertollo's children, unaware that a man was approaching, but the wolf stared at him as Francis snapped twigs underfoot. The wolf met him at the edge of its sanctum. It growled, and something in Francis growled back. The wolf showed its teeth, and Francis crouched and bared his own. The wolf circled Francis and playfully swat him, scratching his arm. Francis was scared, but something within sat him down on the leaves. He closed his eyes and thought deeply, *What is it you want from us?* He repeated the thought in his mind while summoning a howl.

The wolf went down on its belly like a sphinx. Francis kept howling and filling his howl with the thought, *What is it you want from us?* The wolf from its throne of dirt growled and yipped its guttural tones. In the silence that followed, Francis understood the wolf the way someone lost at sea might understand the garbled mew of a whale rising underwater. Francis thought, then howled, "What is it you want?"

The wolf growled, "To return." Francis thought, then howled, "They keep pushing us away…" The wolf howled till its one long note pierced his mind, "I am in Exile!" Francis thought-growled, "I am, too…"

The wolf reared, and facing each other, Francis looked at the wolf's dark center and saw himself. He was on his knees, his animal-spirit howling in his face, and he realized that he fed off the animals the way the wolf fed off the villagers.

The illumination passed, and Francis returned to being a man on his knees in the wilderness before a hungry wolf. He was sweating, in terror of the wolf's strike, but something deeper than his mind reached for the wolf who met his shoulders with its paws and they tumbled: the wolf cutting Francis, he clinging to its fur. As they squirmed, the wolf's spirit entered Francis and his human spirit entered the wolf. Briefly, the man's eyes turned red and the wolf's mind received an inexplicable clarity.

And just as quickly, these gusts of spirit returned, leaving both creatures winded in the dirt. Francis coughed severely, his arms and legs bleeding, wolf fur in his fists. The wolf was panting.

Francis stared through the canopy of trees, overcome by his compassion for the villagers, "It is the hunger they want to kill."

The wolf was licking itself and the more it licked, the more Francis thought of Bertollo and the mayor, "It is the howl they cannot bear."

The wolf seemed smaller. Francis felt larger. He could feel the scratches closing on his arms. He couldn't understand or deny that he was in the wolf, that the wolf was silently howling within him.

7

It took four days, but Francis and the wolf traveled together to the outskirts of Gubbio, and on that edge of wilderness and village, they stopped to feel the wind rush—through the wolf's hair and the fur of Francis's mind. There, like twins in exile, both spirit and wolf felt lonely and free.

As they walked the streets of Gubbio, the silence matched that of the forest. Seeing the scratches all over Francis and the tameness of the wolf, many thought that Francis had overpowered the beast. How could they know that he'd let it in?

Francis brought the wolf to the mayor, who was stunned, "What on earth have you done?"

Francis knelt and embraced the wolf, "This is your brother."

No one could move. The women held their children. The men gripped their weapons. The wolf began to pant as Francis backed away, "This is the emptiness you deny."

The wolf arched its head and let out a howl that broke the seal of many hidden hearts. The men dropped their weapons, and Bertollo's daughter broke a piece of bread and fed it to the beast.

With that, Francis left and the wolf followed Bertollo's daughter home, where it and its den of cubs lived on the offerings of a kinder people.

JOURNAL QUESTIONS

- *It is said that Native Americans value animals because they never forget their original instructions. A bear never forgets what it is to be a bear. But humans forget what it is to be human. Describe one aspect of your original instructions— what it is to be you—and recount your history of understanding this and losing sight of this.*

TABLE QUESTIONS

To be asked over dinner or coffee with friends and loved ones.
Try listening to everyone's response before discussing:

- *Tell the story of one thing you've learned from animals and how you came to learn it.*

- *Tell the story of a time when you felt isolated and alone in your understanding of life.*

A MEDITATION

- *Sit quietly in a public place and meditate on the wolf of Gubbio.*

- *Breathe deeply and reflect on the people's fear of the wolf.*

- *Breathe deeply and consider how the wolf, in being a wolf, mirrored the people's own hunger.*

- *As you exhale, note the people walking by and imagine the people in the buildings about you. Imagine all of us are human animals, needing each other but afraid of each other.*

- *As you inhale, sense the hungers we carry that we project on others.*

- *As you exhale, let go of your own fear of being found out.*

- *As you inhale, welcome your own original instruction.*

- *As you exhale, open your palms and simply welcome being found.*

The Falcon of Truth

THERE IS A POWERFUL MYTH that connects our heartache with the reservoir of universal truth. I'm not sure where it comes from, for it appeared to me in a dream. But the vivid nature of the dream was so convincing it seems clear I am not the first to dream it. In fact, I feel I was allowed to witness something believed and told for generations in some indigenous tribe now forgotten.

In the dream, a godlike falcon sights the opened heart of a man and dives to nibble the piece of heart exposed. The man's pain of living culminates in almost unbearable heartache as the godlike falcon eats that piece of exposed heart. This relieves the man of his heartache, which is replaced by a certain pocket of emptiness—not an emptiness of lack, but a bareness beyond any one person's experience.

It's hard to unravel such a scene in words. We could say that a reward for the open-hearted is that a piece of their heart is forever in the truth that flies over everything. And wherever truth flies, the open-hearted see part of what it sees. And whenever truth opens its wings, no matter what we're doing—sleeping, eating, or churning in our own confusion—an awareness overcomes us momentarily. In time, our piece of heart is mixed with the heartache of others. And so we get back more than just our pain and more than just our own view of truth.

I imagine this deep-seeded myth began when some experienced hunter, waiting in the brush for an antelope to die from its wounds, saw to his amazement a falcon descend with such authority that he tucked himself further in the brush. And there he watched as the lightning bird tore the meat of the wound, and, for a moment, it seemed as if the antelope might rise and run off; but as it dropped, the spirit of the antelope seemed to be in the falcon's mouth. No doubt by the time the hunter's son told his son the story, the antelope did rise and run off while a part of it was forever in the sky with the godlike falcon.

From the earliest times, we have known that opening a wound to air, at some point, is healing. Similarly, when opened by experience, our soul is healed. Yet like a caveman who only dared to leave his wound open because he had nothing to cover it, we await that same moment of undoing. Except for us it takes much longer, since we have endless coverings.

Regardless of whether we are willing or forced, the release of our heartache into the Universe is at once painful and enlightening. Whether we consider this a tragedy or a transformation, to be worn open to truth in this way alleviates some of our pain and bestows in its place a sense of the Infinite, which leaves a sweetness in the world.

JOURNAL QUESTIONS

- *What do you think the relationship is between your personal truth and the truth of the Universe?*

- *Describe one covering—of thought or belief—that is keeping you from a more direct experience of truth.*

TABLE QUESTIONS

To be asked over dinner or coffee with friends and loved ones. Try listening to everyone's response before discussing:

- *Tell the story of one heartache and the piece of truth you've been given for being opened in this way.*

- *Describe one understanding of truth you've been led to that you feel others have understood before you.*

A MEDITATION

- *Sit and center yourself.*

- *As you breathe fully, surface the part of your heart that has most recently been opened.*

- *As you breathe fully, open your arms and welcome the falcon of truth.*

- *As you breathe slowly, let the pain of being opened go. Imagine that the falcon of truth has taken it away.*

- *Close your eyes and feel the empty space left behind.*

- *Breathe into this emptiness and let your mind's eye leave your body to perceive, for the moment, the universal truth from outside of your personal view.*

Cain and Abel

T HEY SECRETLY WANTED THE WHOLE WORLD but falling, as we must, they found themselves each with one berry in their weaker hand. The more stubborn of the two could not let go of his dream, and the berry seemed so small compared to all he wanted. The gap made him bitter. The gentler of the two was shaken into wondering if the dream had led him to this berry, and he was softened further to sense the whole world under its tiny skin.

JOURNAL QUESTIONS

- *Journal an imagined conversation between Cain and Abel about the one berry.*

- *From your own experience, how does comparing lead to bitterness and how does being gentle lead to sensing the whole world?*

TABLE QUESTIONS

To be asked over dinner or coffee with friends and loved ones. Try listening to everyone's response before discussing:

- *Tell the story of the most stubborn person you have known.*

- *Tell the story of the gentlest person you have known.*

- *Who has your ear these days, the Cain in you or the Abel?*

A MEDITATION

- *Meditate with a single berry on a small plate.*

- *Sit quietly with the berry before you and think of all you want in this life.*

- *Breathe in all your dreams and feel your determination. Now hold the berry in your hand as if this is all you'll ever receive. Note what this feels like.*

- *Place the berry back on the plate. Breathe yourself open again. Breathe until you soften. Now hold the same berry in your hand as if this one berry contains everything. Note what this feels like.*

- *Breathe steadily and accept that you have both ways of receiving living within you.*

- *Breathe fully, close your eyes, and eat the berry.*

Keeping the Dish Alive

WHENEVER HE'D TRAVEL TO LANSING, Don would go to a Middle Eastern restaurant he'd stumbled into years ago. He loved their Kibbe Nyah, a dish of freshly ground lamb mixed with herbs and olive oil, seasoned but uncooked. One day, it was off the menu, and Don spoke to the owner, Abu, who said it wasn't worth it. Too few people ordered it. But Don said it was exquisite and pleaded with Abu that the dish shouldn't be lost. Abu said, "You call before you come, and I'll make it for you." So whenever Don would go to Lansing, two or three times a year, he'd call Abu and remind him, "My name is Don. I'm the one who—" But Abu always remembered him, "Yes! Yes! Kibbe Nyah. How are you? Come. I will make it for you." Each time Don would try to tip Abu or pay him extra, but Abu refused, "No. No. Together we keep the dish alive."

After a year, Don asked one of the waiters, "What can I bring Abu?" His old friend smiled and said, "He loves flowers." So the next time Don went to Lansing, he called and Abu said, "Yes. Yes.

Come." And Don walked in with four bouquets of lilies and iris and daffodils. The entire restaurant gathered, clapping and hooting, as Abu wiped his hands on his apron in order to receive the beautiful flowers. The music of his world was turned up and the smell of freshly ground lamb filled the one room and everyone ate with their hands. Abu took stems from the bouquets and placed them around his restaurant. A few of the waiters put iris and daffodils behind each other's ears. Everyone was smiling. And for a long moment, the world seemed right.

JOURNAL QUESTIONS

- *Tell the story of a friendship that grew out of an unexpected kindness.*

TABLE QUESTIONS

To be asked over dinner or coffee with friends and loved ones. Try listening to everyone's response before discussing:

- *Describe one custom or ritual or daily gesture that you have seen practiced that you would like to keep alive. Why?*

- *Tell the story of someone you've seen be kind in an unkind situation.*

A MEDITATION

- *Center yourself and recall a time when you were kind for no reason. It could have been as simple as picking up what a stranger dropped. Or leaving an apple in the path of hungry birds.*

- *Breathe gently and meditate on what being kind feels like.*

- *Breathe deeply and note the difference you feel when you hesitate to give.*

- *Enter your day, not trying to consciously be kind, but rather with a kind outlook that allows you to naturally be who you are and do what you do.*

The Invitation to Grow

"Why is the road to freedom so long?"
asked a troubled apprentice.
And the master replied,
"Because it has to go through you."
—an old Zen story

The Invitation to Grow

I T TAKES YEARS FOR SEEDS TO GROW INTO TREES, and the
seasons shape and scar each tree into place. You could say that
the journey of being a spirit on earth is the human equivalent, and
the years of experience shape and scar each of us into place. You
could say that this is the long road to freedom—inner freedom. It is
our invitation to grow.

When I was starting out, I wanted so badly to become a poet that
I held it in view like some hill I needed to climb to see from. But
getting to the top, something was missing, and so I had to climb the
next hill. Finally, I realized I didn't need to climb to become a poet,
I was a poet.

The same thing happened with love. I wanted so badly to love
and be loved, but climbing through relationships like hills, I realized
again that I was loving and loved all along.

Then I wanted to become wise, but after much travel and study,
it was during my bedridden days with cancer that I realized I was

already wise. I just didn't know the language of my wisdom.

Now I understand that all these incarnations come alive in us when we dare to live the days before us, when we dare to listen to the wind singing in our veins. We carry the love and wisdom like seeds, and the days sprout us. And it's the sprouting that's the poetry. It's the sprouting that's the long road to freedom.

Another lesson is more recent. It comes from a conversation I had with a very wise woman who was a mentor to me. She was the Jungian analyst Helen Luke. I knew Helen during the last two years of her life, and during what turned out to be our last conversation, she said to me, "Yours is to live it, not to reveal it." This troubled me, for I have spent my life becoming a writer, thinking that my job has been just that—to reveal what is essential and hidden.

In the time since Helen died, I've come to understand her last instruction as an invitation to shed any grand purpose, no matter how devoted we may be to what we are doing. She wasn't telling me to stop writing, but to stop striving to be important. She was inviting me to stop *recording* the poetry of life and to *enter* the poetry of life.

This applies to us all. If we devote ourselves to the life at hand, the rest will follow. For life, it seems, reveals itself through those willing to live. Anything else, no matter how beautiful, is just advertising.

This took me many years to learn and accept. Having begun innocently enough there arose separations, and now I know that health resides in restoring direct experience. Thus, having struggled to do what has never been done, I discovered that living is the original art.

The stories in this section speak to the original art of living and how experience keeps asking us to grow.

Tu Fu's Reappearance

OUT OF THE YELLOW MIST HE CAME AGAIN, his Asian beard in tow. We were on a healthy shore, and he sat cross-legged in the sand, scratching delicately with a branch, his slender head down. I crouched and put it to him, "How do I block the fear?" He kept scratching the sand as if he hadn't heard. I grew angry, "How do I block the fear?!" He lifted his head and shrugged, branch waving above him, "How does a tree block the wind?" With that, he disappeared.

JOURNAL QUESTIONS

- *Fear often gets its power from not looking. Share one thing you are currently afraid to look at directly and why.*

TABLE QUESTIONS

To be asked over dinner or coffee with friends and loved ones. Try listening to everyone's response before discussing:

- *This story came in a dream. Tell the story of a dream that has stayed with you and describe what it is drawing your attention to in your life.*

A MEDITATION

- *Breathe cleanly and sit up tall like a bare tree.*

- *As you inhale and exhale, feel the variations of warm and cool pass over your skin like constant winds.*

- *As you inhale, note how only when we hold on to the heat can it lodge as a fever.*

- *As you exhale, note how only when we hold on to the cold can it lodge as a chill.*

- *Breathe cleanly and sit tall like a tree, and note that it is the same with the winds of fear and worry.*

- *As you inhale and exhale, let the myriad things of this life pass near you—the light and dark, the clarity and confusion, the peace and fear, the harmony and chaos—but hold on to none of them.*

- *Breathe cleanly like a tree and let the thousand moods move on through.*

The Desert and the
Marketplace

A SUFI MASTER AND HIS APPRENTICE were traveling across the desert to a marketplace by the sea. Crossing the desert, the apprentice didn't see very much difference between himself and the master. To himself the apprentice mused, *it's not as far to truth as I thought.* But once in the marketplace, the apprentice couldn't take a step clearly. He saw a beautiful woman from afar and wanted to touch her. And wrestling with his desire to touch her, he stopped experiencing her. Now he was fishing in the break of his heart; mourning the last love he'd known, wondering where she was. Then he saw an angry father strike his son and everyone else kept walking by. But he was now feeling his anger at his own father and was no longer experiencing the street. Then, beyond the fish peddlers, a snake handler was dancing his snake in the air and the apprentice was now caught in his mother's fear of snakes. When the master reached for the young man, it was as if he were reaching through a dark fog. The apprentice was startled. The master held his face and said, "When you can walk the city like a desert and the desert like a city, the sun will be your heart above you and your heart will be the sun inside you."

JOURNAL QUESTIONS

- *Being human, we are easily clouded by a fog of associations that keep us from direct experience.*
  - *Give a recent example of when you, like the apprentice, were jettisoned from the moment you were experiencing into your own parallel world.*
  - *Give the history of this one association and where it lives in you presently.*

TABLE QUESTIONS

To be asked over dinner or coffee with friends and loved ones. Try listening to everyone's response before discussing:
- *Tell the story of a fear you have inherited.*
- *The master concludes that "When you can walk the city like a desert and the desert like a city, the sun will be your heart above you and your heart will be the sun inside you." What do you think this means?*

A MEDITATION

- *Meditate, if you can, in public. On a bench or in a café or near a window where people are passing.*

- *As you center yourself, begin to inhale and exhale and let you and the world enter each other.*

- *As you breathe slowly, note the difference between the things outside of you—gestures, voices, noises, shadows—and the things inside of you—feelings, thoughts, memories, questions.*

- *As you breathe deeply, let your associations arise and let them settle.*

- *As you breathe cleanly, let the things outside of you begin to return to what they are.*

- *As you breathe cleanly, let the things inside of you begin to settle like sand on the bottom.*

- *This will take some time and will, no doubt, require further meditation. Revisit this practice, if you are so moved.*

Seeds Within Seeds

THEY LIVED IN THE SMALL VILLAGE of Badaling, at the foot of the mountains whose waters feed the Luan River to the east. It is said that the songs of these simple people have carried for centuries along the Luan all the way to the great Bo Hai Sea where they lure the fish to the surface. Zhang was a master gardener who worked for the general who ran the village. Zhang had long been deep friends with the general's wife, Shenji. And both had befriended the gentle drifter Li Bai, who appeared last spring.

The three of them were meeting, as had become their habit, in the upper part of the garden, near the old gazebo. Zhang had built that gazebo years ago with Shenji's father. It was a private, holy place. Zhang was just beginning to say something to Shenji when Li Bai arrived.

Zhang motioned for him to sit, "I was just about to tell Shenji about a thought that has saved my life. It's not my thought, but that of Mencius, the grandson of the great Confucius. It's the kind of thought that no one owns, but he was the one to give it voice, over a thousand years ago. I count myself blessed to have heard it.

"What Mencius said was that human beings are innately kind, that we are born open and giving. He spoke of this kindness as a form of water. He said if allowed its natural course, all water will flow downhill and, though we can manipulate it to flow uphill, its natural want is to flow through crevices, all the way to the sea. Likewise, when allowed our natural course, we will always be kind, and, though circumstances can manipulate us to be otherwise, our natural want is to let our kindness flow through the emptiness of others.

"There have been times in my life when I have been so broken that I could do nothing but wait for the kindness of others to flow through me. And having known that deep water, this great idea has given me strength to be what I was born to be—kind."

Both Shenji and Li Bai sat in wonder at what came from Zhang, for he had no formal education. It was even unclear how he had learned to read. He would only say that being a gardener had made him a flower. Their thoughts were now on him and not on what Mencius had said. The old gardener could sense this, and so he quickly shifted the conversation, "But I, too, suffer the changes around me. It never ends. For instance, look at this."

Zhang pulled out a small bag filled with black, almond-shaped seeds. He poured some on the ground, "These seeds come all the way from Africa." Shenji was having trouble keeping up, for her heart was agitated, but she picked up a seed, "What will they grow into?" Zhang admitted, "I don't know. But they pose a problem for me. I need your advice."

This confused Shenji, for she was still in the other conversation. But she settled in to listen to Zhang as he scooped a handful of the unknown seeds and continued, "The General gave them to me. He said they were sent along by the Emperor's son, Ti. At first, I thought this very considerate. And part of me can't wait till spring to see what small miracle sprouts from the earth."

He opened his palm filled with the dark seeds, "All the way from Africa." He let them spill back to the ground, "But then, I've heard such awful things about Ti and his father. And this is my question: Should I plant them or not? Will Ti's touch poison the garden? Or is the seed stronger than the one who bears it?"

Shenji's heart was pounding, "Don't plant them." Li Bai pressed her, "Why? What have you heard?" "Nothing, really. I just know that Ti is a heartless man." Li Bai wondered aloud, "But if we only plant what comes from clean hands, the earth will be barren." Zhang laughed, but Shenji became edgy, "I just don't feel good about this." They all grew silent until Zhang rose from a place of deep thought, "It all depends on whether the seed rubs off on the man or the man rubs off on the seed, doesn't it?"

All this talk seemed idle to Shenji, who saw the seeds as a calamity about to happen. She looked at the seeds waiting there between them, and felt as if the two of them were talking about the nature of water while a fire was spreading. She stood and kicked the pile of seeds, yelling, "They will poison the garden!" Zhang was shocked and went to comfort her, "Shenji, please, please, there. I would never do anything to jeopardize all this. It holds my life." And Shenji began to cry.

While Zhang held her, Li Bai could see that Shenji was frightened about the dangers building in her house, and he could see that Zhang was going to plant the seeds as a matter of faith.

It was the first time Zhang had seen Shenji raise her voice. She was calming down and something in Li Bai's presence settled them into another deep silence. Zhang sighed deeply. He would do anything for Shenji. All this only affirmed his impulse to plant the unknown seeds. He thought it a covenant to wait till spring to see what unknown colors would sprout from the earth.

Shenji seemed exhausted now. She laid on the grass and began to doze. Li Bai cautioned himself. It was a mistake to take sides. He spread himself on the ground and watched the sky and dozed off, too.

When he woke, Shenji was still napping, but Zhang was spinning slowly in a dance of Chi about a spot of newly dug earth east of the gazebo. He watched Zhang for a while and knew he'd planted the seeds while they slept. When Zhang noticed him, the old gardener laughed in a whisper as he kept dancing, "I've never been happier than in this moment together." He kept spinning, "All the times I have known, all the feelings I have felt, all the silences in my mind— all are here now in this dance."

Li Bai was dumbstruck, for the old gardener was aglow. Somehow, by planting the innocent seeds that had come from heartless hands, he seemed invulnerable to dark influences. He had found some seam in eternity. He was—in this instant—pure joy. He was old and young at once.

JOURNAL QUESTIONS

- *Both Shenji and Li Bai fall asleep before the difficult question of whether to plant the seeds or not. And while they sleep, the master gardener plants the seeds and discovers joy. What does Zhang stay awake to that the others do not?*

- *If all three characters live in you, what parts of you do they represent?*

TABLE QUESTIONS

To be asked over dinner or coffee with friends and loved ones. Try listening to everyone's response before discussing:

- *Describe a moment of giving when the character of the giver somehow tainted the gift.*

- *Describe a moment of giving when the character of the gift somehow cleansed the giver.*

- *Discuss the difference.*

- *Are you carrying any seeds that you're unsure about planting? How have they come to you? What is your hesitation in planting them?*

A MEDITATION

- *Choose something that you want to grow and choose something that you want to put to rest, that you want to bury. It can be an actual seed or a symbolic one. You could even write what each is on a piece of paper.*

- *Close your eyes and hold each in your hands, deep in your palms.*

- *Breathe deeply and thank what you want to bury for what it has opened in you, though it may have been painful.*

- *Breathe fully and thank what you want to plant for its capacity to regenerate.*

- *Take what you want to bury and what you want to plant outside, and place each, side by side, in the earth. If you can't go outside, place each, side by side, in the same pot of soil.*

- *Close your eyes and feel that both are covered by the same earth.*

- *Breathe steadily and feel the earth on your hands.*

- *With each breath, reflect on the difference between burying and planting.*

The Translator's Son

The Father

HIS FATHER KNEW that words once contained more: the way ancient tents used their one great space for eating, cleaning, sleeping, not yet divided into kitchen, bathroom, bedroom. His father learned Swahili at the age of fifty because of a legend. It seems a tribe had charged its elders to name the spirit behind everything. After several years, each returned with a different name, and the Shaman tied them together with a twine of honeyed smoke; forbidding them to break the circle until they forged one name.

By the end of the rainy season, when the unseen falls at the jungle's core hiss and roar, they emerged with the word. Some say the elders would never share it and the Shaman, in revenge, split their speech. Some believe their split versions of the word gave rise to the different names for God. Others believe that the Shaman enchanted each to carry their piece of the one name forever, and only when given to each other freely will the spirit behind everything appear. His father always quipped, "A good translator, like a Shaman, tries to empower strangers to speak the lost and common name for God."

The Son

As if birth were a translation, he carried his father's wish. When six, he watched a snake slither from the bank, moving without really moving. He felt the imprint of its belly in the dirt and knew the fate of words. He couldn't touch its path in the water and knew the fate of feelings.

As he grew, people for no reason would share their genesis of pain, their spurts and fatigues, their rigidity and doubt. They'd look into his eyes and display their shards of fear and he—it seemed quite natural—would fit them to each other. A singer with a love for cats to a lawyer with a litter. A fisherman tired of casting with a sentimental florist.

His father wanted him to master Swahili. But he learned Russian and French and went to work in the UN behind one of those glass booths, his soft voice flooding anonymously through foreign inner ears.

He was hired for the Nuclear Summit at the time his father took ill. It softened his indifference, stirred his mushroom-cloud dreams. He folded his laundry, reciting the Russian phonemes for Nuclear.

His father was failing, though still searching for the word. It saddened him, and so in between the talks, he walked through department stores, watching the stacks of TVs all turned to the same

channel. Sixty women with the same teeth, smiling. His father's whole
life chasing a word. Flash. The News. Sixty times the latest home
Exploded. Exploded. All the different names for God. Exploded.
Flash. Sixty birds gliding over water, gliding, gliding, as the salesman
approached, "Are you interested in high-quality resolution?"

His reputation for detached excellence made him the one for the
President and Premier. After slow negotiations, they entered once
more and bowed like dark elders. The President said, "We can no
longer tolerate your position." He smiled and passed it on, "We can
no longer tolerate the danger." The Premier responded, "Only if
you disarm first, can we proceed." He smiled in his glass booth and
passed it on, "Only if we disarm together, can we proceed." The first
was off-balance, "How can we trust you?" He smiled and passed it
on, "We have no choice but to trust you." The other came undone,
"Do you really mean this?" He encircled them with raw language,
threading their responses till they forged a common peace.

Of course, he was discovered and dismissed. But he did it for his
father, and in that moment of agreement, however false, he felt like
a Shaman, and the leaders, briefly, felt like unappointed elders intent
on mastering the whole.

JOURNAL QUESTIONS

- *Try to describe your history with the presence of spirit and the different names you've given this experience along the way.*

TABLE QUESTIONS

To be asked over dinner or coffee with friends and loved ones. Try listening to everyone's response before discussing:

- *Tell the story of someone you admire as a bridger or translator. It might be someone you know or someone from history.*

- *Though it remains impossible, try as a group, like the elders in the story, to share your names for the spirit behind everything. Once listening to each other, try to forge one name that has meaning for all of you.*

A MEDITATION

- *Close your eyes and listen to all that is around you.*

- *Breathe steadily and listen for what is under what you hear.*

- *Open your eyes and know that to listen to what has meaning under everything is to be a bridge of being.*

- *Enter your day ready to listen for where you can be a bridge among living things.*

Crossing Time

DESPITE HIS AGE, HE WAS TALKING FAST, excited about those long gone, about their greatness and courage. Since I'd never heard of them, his eyes became a window to another world. Each name unstitched a story too complex to convey, too searing to leave alone. He sipped his tea and I realized that I will speak of him this way.

We talked long into the night, and he started to drift. I moved his cane and touched his shoulder and he smiled his way back to now. I said, "Shall we go?" He whispered, "We're already gone." Then slapped his knee, "But it's all right."

I bent over to help him up when he held my head with both his hands and kissed my forehead. He then put his palm firmly on my chest and said, "You know." As we waited for his car, he smelled a weed like a flower and sighed. And still I wonder what it is I know.

JOURNAL QUESTIONS

- *Bring to mind someone in your personal history or in world history that you have always admired, and, though you might know the events of their time on earth, look into the story of who they were as a person. Then, enlist them as a guide, and journal an imagined conversation with them.*

TABLE QUESTIONS

To be asked over dinner or coffee with friends and loved ones. Try listening to everyone's response before discussing:

- *Is there someone in your life now who you will speak about as great and courageous in years to come? What is their story?*
- *Speak about someone in history that you feel a connection to. Describe that connection and how you discovered it. It can be the person you write about in your journal.*
- *What does "he smelled a weed like a flower and sighed" mean to you?*

A MEDITATION

- *Sit calmly and put your palm firmly on your own chest.*
- *Breathe slowly and cleanly with your eyes closed.*

- *Feel whatever it is that flows from your heart to your palm and back.*

- *Do this each morning for at least three days and reflect each day on what it is you know that is incorruptible and life-affirming.*

Wisdom of the Chew

I T WAS SOMETHING UNFORGIVABLE. This much he was sure of. It was many years ago. He'd crossed the sea to this island and though his father knew where he was, he never came. But it was important to get away. To grow in his own light. Though since, he's learned it's everyone's light.

At first, he built a hut with only one window, and every noise issued a fear. A native who became his teacher broke the east wall down. Now the outside was in and he could see the sun rise. In six months, most of his fears went away.

His teacher took him into the forest where they gathered roots and herbs. They turned them into a healing paste they gave away. When alone, he rubbed the paste on his own heart, but it only dulled the pain that was his father.

One day while gathering roots, he was surrounded by the chew of giraffes in the tops of slender trees. He simply listened to the wisdom of their chew. One looked at him as if to say: *To chew small things that make it to the light, this is worth sticking your neck out.*

After that, he took the west wall down. Now he could see the light come and go. It was from the west that he saw a small lighted thing bob on the sea. As it came closer, he could tell it was a man in a boat. At first, the back of his heart, where he kept his father, jumped behind his eyes, and he thought: *At last, he has come.*

The boat disappeared in each wave. Close enough and he could see a stranger rowing. The image of his father slouched back into the corner of his heart. The stranger told him that his father was dying. He went into the forest to be with the giraffes who had no advice. He leaned against a tree and pulled at his long flowing beard. He thanked the stranger and sent him off.

A week later, he began to row back over the years and couldn't remember why he left. No doubt, it was something important, something stifling enough that he needed to go. He kept rowing through the waves that had brought him to his life and halfway between who he'd become and who he was, he drifted.

His father had died; he could feel it. And the wind, his constant friend, held its breath in sadness. He began pulling his hands through the tangles of his beard. For a moment, the vast water went still and he could see himself. He had become his father. The only way to love him now was to love himself.

JOURNAL QUESTIONS

- *Tell the story of a time when you felt wounded or betrayed by another and how your view of this event has changed over time.*

- *Journal an imagined conversation with the person who hurt you.*

TABLE QUESTIONS

To be asked over dinner or coffee with friends and loved ones. Try listening to everyone's response before discussing:

- *Tell the story of a time when you hurt someone and where the pain of hurting someone lives in you.*

- *It is no mistake that to digest things, we have to chew on them. Given this, what do you think the title, "Wisdom of the Chew" means?*

A MEDITATION

- *As you sit, center yourself, and for this brief meditation, know it is safe for the hurt you have experienced and the hurt you have caused to show itself.*

- *Breathe gently on the pain that arises, whether caused or received.*

- *As you inhale, note how similar all hurt is, once free of all cause and effect.*

- *As you exhale, let these hurts merge.*

- *As you breathe gently, bring into view one person who has hurt you and one person you have hurt.*

- *As you breathe gently, imagine them on either side of you.*

- *As you breathe slowly and gently, imagine all three of you letting go of the hurts that bind you.*

Facing a Demon

A LARGE DEMON APPEARED IN THE VILLAGE ONE DAY. Out of fear, the blacksmith poked its cheek with his hot iron and the demon ate him. With the wound on his face, the demon seemed scarier. All the men started to carry weapons. This made the demon more cunning and more ferocious. Two brothers decided to hunt the demon. One was a dancer. The other, a butcher. When they found the demon, the dancer distracted it with his dance, while the butcher went to slice its throat. The demon ate them both.

In desperation, the mayor of the village went to the old shaman for advice. He was so old that he was losing his sight. While people pitied him, he considered his slow loss of sight a protection of sorts. He said it kept him from misusing his gifts. When the mayor explained what had happened, the shaman said, "The dancer misused his dance. The butcher misused his knife. And the blacksmith misused his iron. Now the demon is stronger, and it embodies the grace of a dancer, the skill of a butcher, and the strength of a blacksmith."

The mayor and the people felt defeated. It was then that the shaman offered his secret, "You must feed it light and wait."

Fear sapped the kindness of the village. In their growing agitation, they beseeched a gentle young monk, the one who as a boy would cry if he stepped on an ant. They gave him a dagger of light and pleaded with him to face the demon. The young monk, who was privately unsure whether to keep his vows or launch headlong into the world, said yes.

He sat at the edge of the forest, with the dagger of light on his lap, and waited. On the third day, the demon, hungry and frightened, appeared. The demon had been cut so many times by swords that the sight of even a lighted dagger made it growl and rear. To the demon's surprise, the young man quickly swallowed the dagger of light, as the shaman had instructed. It cut him on the way down. He stilled himself and waited. The demon waited. And then, the demon spread prone on the earth and opened its mouth like the gates to another world.

The gentle young man could feel the dagger of light move inside him. Though weakened, he carefully rose and entered the demon, walking through the gates of its mouth down the tunnel of its throat. Once in its belly, he heard desperate voices pleading to be released. Once his eyes adjusted to the dark, he could see the butcher in the corner, and the blacksmith, and the dancer. They were trembling. Then, in the center of the demon's belly, a raw and tearful being approached him. But instead of hurting him, the being began to plead, "At last, can you save me?! Please! You must get me out of here!"

The young monk sat before his darker self and said, "I have entered your belly. You must enter mine." At once, the frightened being trapped in the belly of the demon understood and reached down the young monk's throat to pull the dagger of light from *his* belly. It cut the young monk's innocence and he passed out.

The frightened being trapped in the belly of the demon lifted the dagger of light. And with the strength of a blacksmith and the skill of a butcher and the grace of a dancer, the frightened, trapped being stabbed the demon from inside. The opening let in the light, the unending light, and the demon's body shriveled and vanished, leaving them all as they were the day they were consumed—the same but changed.

JOURNAL QUESTIONS

- *The story suggests that a demon is some aspect of a situation that we enlarge and empower by how we feel about it and think about it.*

- *Describe a situation that is currently very large and troubling for you and your attempts to silence it or thwart it.*

- *Trace the origin of this situation when it was smaller and how it has grown large and troubling.*

- *Imagine that in the center of this large and troubling thing there is something raw and tearful which, if given the chance, might say, "At last, can you save me?" Journal an imagined conversation with the raw and tearful thing in the center of your demon.*

TABLE QUESTIONS

To be asked over dinner or coffee with friends and loved ones. Try listening to everyone's response before discussing:

- *In the story, the shaman says that the dancer, the butcher, and the blacksmith misused their gifts. How so? What is your understanding of this?*
- *Describe a time when you misused one of your gifts.*

A MEDITATION

- *Sit calmly and breathe slowly.*
- *As you inhale, imagine that you are safe, behind a clear glass wall.*
- *As you exhale, close your eyes and imagine something or some-one behind the clear glass wall that frightens you.*
- *As you breathe steadily, let your rush of fear come and go. Do nothing. You are safe.*
- *As you inhale, note how your fear enlarges what you see. Do nothing. You are safe.*
- *As you exhale, note how your safety right-sizes what you see. Do nothing. You are safe.*
- *Breathe slowly and have compassion for what you fear.*

Hands Like Wings

FROM AN EARLY AGE, Cheryl thought hands were like wings searching for a way to fly. So naturally, when she started to sculpt, she made the hands bigger. Her mother assumed that big hands meant they were angels. Cheryl will tell you that her angels are meant to be mounted on walls. They seem to rise out of whatever wall they find themselves on, the way the deeper self arises no matter what impediment we grow in its way. Her sculptures seem to have a life of their own. She releases them more than creates them and so has never felt particularly attached to them. Except for one. Her sculpture of Sophia. This one felt like it had arisen from behind her own wall. It was no surprise that this sculpture drew everyone. Wherever she'd show it, people would quietly start to touch the overlarge hands, then touch their lips. Some would touch their lips first. Quietly, when no one was looking, her angel of Sophia began to bless those who reached for her.

Sophia came to Cheryl after her mother died. When the grief would get too heavy to bear, Sophia would flutter between the weight of it and the sculptor's tired heart. She never knew this, but it was after the weight of her grief fluttered that the presence of such a sculpture awakened in her.

About six years ago, she was asked to mount an exhibit in the local hospital. Her flock of angels with overlarge hands arose from the walls offering grace to the sick and lame and those rushing around helping everyone. She never knew the full impact of her angels. She just knew that hanging such a show in a hospital seemed absolutely right.

The show had been up three months when Cheryl got a call. One of the angels was gone. Her immediate fear came true. It was Sophia. Of all her pieces, why Sophia? The only one she needed. The one she loved the most. Her first feeling was one of fear and emptiness, as if the secret of her creativity came from Sophia. How could she continue without her? It was raining that day, and as she drove to the hospital, she felt that a deep part of her had been violated. The wipers squeaked as they kept clearing small pelts of water from the sky.

As she raced past the emergency room, her other angels said nothing. Her heart was pounding. Turning the corner toward out-patient surgery, she saw the empty wall. It was quiet and no one seemed to notice. Everyone was busy being ill, being afraid, wanting help, fearing help, caring for each other, and feeling overworked. She stood and stared at the empty wall for a long time.

The art therapist who had arranged the show arrived and was

very apologetic, "I can't imagine who would steal an angel." An old man with a walker overheard and muttered, "Someone desperate for grace." No one heard him. And no one was sure what to do. Cheryl was heartbroken. The art therapist somehow felt responsible. Soon a hospital administrator arrived. He was thoughtful but impatient. They walked to the security office where a young man in blue brought up tapes on a camera from the night before. He was fast-forwarding to the suspicious part. It seemed odd to Cheryl, watching the lives of others speed by just as life was standing still for her.

"There," said the young man in blue. He backed up the tape. In the empty hall, a thin man with Sophia over his shoulder was slipping across the bottom of the screen. The blue man froze the scene. The numbers in the corner read 10:43 PM. It was impossible to see his face. He had a bulky jacket on. But there was Sophia, her fluttering eyes staring at Cheryl through the camera, her large hands on the thief's back.

Don's heart was breaking. He had never taken anything in his life, not even candy as a boy. But his mother had just died before his eyes and he was spinning, groundless, feeling desperate and alone. The weight of this angel on his shoulder was a comfort. From an early age, Don had a special closeness with his mother. She was a kind force in the world, as quiet and steady as a sunny day. No matter the harshness that life would present, Don could retreat into the force of his mother's kindness and repair. What kept Don from himself was how he hid in his mother's kindness rather than gaining strength from it. This kept him from finding the force of kindness in his own soul.

Don was never good with people, though he liked to be around people. He never married and wound up managing a local diner. He was in his forties when his mother began to fail. She never wanted him to circle her as he did, but she thanked God for his devotion. She had Parkinson's, and over time her limitations grew. Don would always tuck her in and she would motion to him just as he neared the door. Without a word, she'd smile like the sun itself and cup his cheek. This small moment became Don's rosary. It kept him going.

There were no siblings and no intimate friends. So as Don's mother failed, she became like a beautiful coastline reclaimed by the sea. Whole parts of her were no longer visible, except to Don in the shrine of his love. About eighteen months ago, it was discovered that his mother had cancer. The journey, already difficult, became overwhelming. For the last six weeks, she was hospitalized.

Of all the people in the world, Don thought, why her? The only one he needed. The one he loved the most. Now his first feeling every day was one of fear and emptiness, as if the secret of his ability to live came from his mother's kindness. How could he continue without her? It was raining the day that she would die, and as he drove to the hospital, he felt that a deep part of him was being violated.

He knew something was different the moment he entered her room. She seemed to dim before his eyes. Her kindness was there, but faint, like a song suddenly heard through a pillow. He leaned close to her all day. Finally, in the evening, when the nurses were elsewhere, she looked to him. But she was too weak to cup his face. She simply smiled at him and died with her eyes open, her kindness streaming at him like a sun he couldn't prevent from setting.

He had no idea how long he stayed there. Life had torn open and some bottomless place he'd kept hidden was screaming silently within him. He felt desperate to run from it. Of course, he couldn't. He couldn't stop staring into those eyes that had sent kindness to him his whole life. When he let go of her dead hand, it seemed larger than in life. He backed out of the room into a world without her.

In the hall, nurses were chatting about overtime and doses of medicine, and one fanned herself with a chart. Someone asked him how she was doing. He walked right by her, unable to speak. How could he continue? Where would he go? Everything seemed insignificant. He wandered about the hospital, trying to catch his breath. He was afraid to cry, afraid if he let that flood begin, he'd drown there in the hall. The shock was making him weak. He was buckling at the knees. He braced himself against the wall.

When he looked up, there was a sculpture of his mother with her dead, large hands. And there were her dead eyes, which had sent kindness his whole life. How was this possible? He stroked Sophia's face and touched her large hands. He began to sob. He felt, for the moment, that if he let go of this angel, he'd be lost forever. He backed away and felt terrified, out of control. He fell back against the wall and cupped his hand on the angel's face, the way his mother cupped his face. He stood there for a long time, his hand on the sculpture mounted on the wall. It felt like a raft in the storm.

Don couldn't go back into the world and he couldn't stay there. He was sobbing and drowning, and the only thing his broken heart could think of was to take the sudden angel with him. At least for a while. He had never taken anything in his life, not even candy as a boy. But his mother had just died before his eyes and he was spinning, groundless, feeling desperate and alone. The weight of this angel on his shoulder was a comfort.

Cheryl never knew who had stolen her angel. And though she never saw the tape from the security camera again, the image of the thin man with Sophia over his shoulder slipping across the bottom of the screen was imprinted in her mind. Six years have passed and Cheryl has come to see Sophia's sudden absence as a teacher. She admits in quiet moments that she was heartbroken for a long time. Then, somehow, she realized that Sophia was alive within her. Somehow, Cheryl was forced to see need as a messenger of light. She still coaxes hands into their largeness, still invites angels to rise through walls. To no one in particular, she admits that all this has made her a better artist. She will tell you that kindness flows from living thing to living thing. "We only borrow it," she says. Then she chuckles, "Or rather, kindness borrows us."

Don is still not very good with people, but managing the diner keeps his loneliness at bay. And every morning, as he leaves his apartment, he reaches for the table near his small window and cups the angel's face and touches her large hands. Doing this, he feels strong enough to enter the world.

He has no idea that in a few days, the sun will come out and he will feel a kindness at work in the world that he hasn't felt since his mother died. He has no way of knowing that he will stop on the way to work at the edge of a small park to watch a pair of chickadees peck through the snow for fallen seed. He has no way of knowing that as he watches the small birds feed, Cheryl will be waking slowly from a dream in which she has become Sophia. At that moment, Don will sit on a snow-wet bench and close his eyes before the warmth of the sun and briefly he will feel whole again, ready to live. He will wake the next day, no longer needing the stolen angel. And too ashamed to return her, he will start looking for a place to leave her, to thank her, to bless the sculptor he will never know.

But today, as Don shuffles to work, the early light through his small window falls on Sophia's large hands. As she waits for someone else to create her. For someone else to steal her. Waiting for who will need her next.

JOURNAL QUESTIONS

- *Imagine that you are interviewing Cheryl and Don separately.*

- *What would you ask each about how this experience has changed them?*

- *What would each offer as their understanding of how to live through the heartbreak of loss?*

- *Journal these conversations.*

TABLE QUESTIONS

To be asked over dinner or coffee with friends and loved ones.
Try listening to everyone's response before discussing:

- *Toward the end of the story, Cheryl remarks "that kindness flows from living thing to living thing. 'We only borrow it,' she says. Then she chuckles, 'Or rather, kindness borrows us.'" What do these insights suggest about the nature of kindness and our relationship to it?*

- *What do you make of Cheryl's heartbreak at having her favorite sculpture stolen and the absolute healing of how her art keeps another alive through their suffering?*

- *What does this story say about the purpose of art?*

A MEDITATION

- *This is a meditation to be entered with a loved one.*

- *Sit facing each other and breathe quietly.*

- *Once centered, hold each other's hands.*

- *Breathe slowly and focus on each other's hands.*

- *With each inhalation, try to feel the love flowing to you.*

- *With each exhalation, try to feel the love flowing from you.*

- *After a time, drop the other's hands and look at your own.*

- *Breathe steadily and feel your hands enlarge with the pulse of love.*

Feeling Small

THE OTHER DAY, I WAS FEELING SMALL. I needed to get away. So I went to the city. And everyone looked familiar, like I'd seen them before. I went up to one man and said, "Don't I know you?" He turned and said, "What are you lookin' at?" And I said, "Oh, I thought I saw God in your eyes." Just then, the woman passing behind us stopped and said, "No, it was me." And we embraced. Then the first man said, "Hey! Wait! Can I come, too?" And we all embraced. And the wind slipping through our legs on the street sounded just like the rush of life.

JOURNAL QUESTIONS

- *Describe a time when you sensed a true familiarity with someone you didn't really know that well.*

- *What kind of relationship developed from this unexplained familiarity, if any?*

- *How do you understand this phenomenon?*

TABLE QUESTIONS

To be asked over dinner or coffee with friends and loved ones. Try listening to everyone's response before discussing:

- *Describe a time when looking at something with others opened up an understanding that you couldn't have arrived at alone.*

- *In our age, people are so estranged from themselves and isolated from each other that it's difficult to discern when it's safe to reach out to others, and yet we so desperately need the balm of community. How do we make our way? What skills are necessary to find each other? What can we do in our day-to-day lives?*

A MEDITATION

- *Close your eyes and reflect on your own sense of isolation, how you are separate from others in the hive of modern life.*

- *Inhale slowly and let that inhalation draw you toward the center of your being.*

- *Once feeling your center, breathe fully and reflect on your sense of commonness with all living things, how at center we are all connected.*

- *Breathe steadily and feel the crossover, back and forth, between your connectedness and your isolation. Feel how both are true.*

- *As you move through your day, note which takes charge of your awareness, your isolation or your connectedness.*

- *As you encounter each, try to discern in your heart how accurate each instance is or if one is echoing into the other.*

- *At the end of the day, close your eyes and allow both your isolation and your connectedness to mingle in the unnamable center of your being.*

The Illumination

ALISON'S GRANDMOTHER ANNA IS 103. She lives in a retire-
ment village. Alison is one of eight grandchildren, and she has
learned that her grandmother, at one time or another, has told each
they are her favorite. Through the years, Anna has showered each of
them with an unrestrained love that has illuminated their special-
ness. Far from feeling misled, Alison feels grateful for how endless
her grandmother's love has been. When Alison visits her grandmother now, it's clear that Anna can no longer retain who people are
or how she knows them. Even when she does, she doesn't remember
for long. Now everyone is a stranger and everyone is her favorite.
Everyone is special.

Alison settles into a peaceful place of awe as she tells me this.
"Now it's just pure love," she says, "for everyone and everything."
Alison shakes her head and smiles, "Grandma's love is no longer
reserved for family because everyone has become family." It is pro-
found and humbling that it should take a hundred years to find our
way to this. Can there be any greater ambition?

JOURNAL QUESTIONS

- *Tell the story of a relative who welcomed a stranger into your family and how your family reacted.*

- *Describe a time when you were unexpectedly made to feel like family by someone other than family.*

TABLE QUESTIONS

To be asked over dinner or coffee with friends and loved ones. Try listening to everyone's response before discussing:

- *What have you found liberating as well as confining about family?*

- *Under what circumstances would you enlarge your sense of family?*

A MEDITATION

- *Close your eyes and open yourself to the history of your family, known and unknown.*

- *Breathe slowly and imagine your great-grandmother being helped in another land by a stranger. Maybe she fell and was helped up. Maybe she lost her way and was put back on her path.*

- *Inhale deeply and imagine that stranger's family making its way through time to this country.*

- *Exhale deeply and imagine that stranger's great-granddaughter is someone you will meet today.*

- *Breathe slowly and be ready to help her as her family once helped yours.*

- *Open your eyes and enter the day ready to be kind to everyone you meet, because you won't know who she is.*

Blessedly

AFTER A LARGE SNOWFALL, a young poet came to my door. He seemed a younger version of myself. After a while, he finally asked about greatness and fame. He was wild-eyed, and underneath everything everyone had told him to strive for, I could see his snow-like soul.

So I said, "Let's go for a walk." I put on my boots as my dog jumped in the car, and we drove to a pine forest that few knew of. He talked the whole way.

We hiked the perimeter at first, and I listened until he ran out of words. Our steps slowed, and I hoped he would see that we were on a path that someone had cleared before he was born.

My dog kept running ahead, then looking back, to make sure we were coming. Now neither of us said a word.

When we entered the rows of sixty-foot pines, we could hear the tops creak, and I hoped he would see that we were in a forest that someone had planted long before I was born.

My dog led us off the path till we came upon a cross made of broken limbs, staked between the pines. It was covered with snow, the way pain if left in the open is softened by prayer.

It seemed obvious that we would never know who had staked the cross or who had planted the pines or who had cleared the path. Our cold breath clouded and merged, and I smiled deeply to know that this is how it is.

On the way back, I was lost in the crunch of my boots in the snow. When I stopped, he was fifty yards back, watching me get smaller. It was then I knew he understood. So I turned and kept walking into the white field that covered all names.

JOURNAL QUESTIONS

- *Describe a time when you were working hard to be seen and what that experience led to, and a time when you were working hard to see and what that led to.*

- *In a world obsessed with being seen and with celebrity more than seeing and celebrating, what's the difference?*

TABLE QUESTIONS

To be asked over dinner or coffee with friends and loved ones. Try listening to everyone's response before discussing:

• *Tell the story of an anonymous path you have walked, or an anonymous tool you have used, or an anonymous teaching that has guided you.*

• *What would you say to those who created these gifts, if you could?*

A MEDITATION

• *Breathe calmly and know that the air that keeps you alive remains unseen.*

• *Breathe slowly and know that the wind that lifts an eagle gets no applause.*

• *Breathe deeply and know that the light that makes the corn grow gets no award.*

• *Sit quietly and reflect on something worthwhile that you have done that no one knows about. Note what this feels like.*

• *Feel your kinship to the air that keeps you alive, the wind that lifts, and the light that makes things grow.*

• *Breathe deeply and feel the center of your being that lives below all names.*

Notes

The Cover: "Canyon," an original woodblock by Mary Brodbeck. Mary is my woodblock teacher. She is remarkably talented and kind. Since 1998, Mary has specialized in *moku hanga*–woodblock prints made using all traditional Japanese methods and materials. She learned these techniques from Yoshisuke Funasaka in Tokyo, as a recipient of a Bunka-Cho fellowship from the Japanese government. Mary's exhibits her work throughout the United States, Canada, and Japan. For more about Mary and her work, please visit www.MaryBrodbeck.com.

p. xi, dedication: "For everyone who ever carried a story . . ." written by the author.

p. xiii, epigraph one: "A story must be told in such a way . . ." from *Meetings*, Martin Büber. Chicago, IL: Open Court Press, 1991.

p. 3, Staying Close: ". . . the courage to listen to your own life . . . the abiding commitment to respect your own and others' journeys . . ." I am indebted to the generosity of John Paul Lederach, a visionary in the peace-building movement, who invited me to lead a Poetry & Peace-building Retreat for his students at Notre Dame. The retreat was held twice in March 2007 and in April 2010. In preparing for this, we discovered that to be a poet and a peace-builder requires at heart the same devotions of inner attention mentioned above. Please see *The Moral Imagination* and *The Journey Toward Reconciliation,* both by John Paul Lederach.

p. 7, On and Off the Path, section epigraph: "The world is not comprehensible . . ." from *Meetings*, Martin Büber. Chicago, IL: Open Court Press, 1991.

p. 21, The Tea Master and the Warrior: "Rikiu . . . and Taiko . . ." In sixteenth-century Japan, Rikiu was one of the great tea masters whose long friendship with the warrior-prince Taiko-Hideyishi was legendary. After many years, a jealous treachery arose toward Rikiu and when a distance grew between Taiko and Rikiu, the enemies of the tea master spread rumors that Rikiu was going to poison Taiko with a cup of tea. Hearing this rumor, Taiko coldly discounted their long friendship and without any further inquiry condemned Rikiu to die by his own hand. Surrounded by his students, Rikiu offered them all a final cup of tea and ended the tea ceremony by breaking the sacred cup to keep it from being misused by others. He then whispered, "Welcome O sword of eternity . . . Through Buddha thou has cleft the way" and fell on his dagger. To learn more about the tea ceremony and the reverent way of life behind it, see the classic *The Book of Tea* by Okakura-Kakuzo. It is also of interest that *Taiko* means *drum* in Japanese. In feudal Japan, a *taiko* was often used to motivate troops and call out orders. Entering a battle, the *taiko yaku* (drummer) was responsible for setting the pace of the march.

p. 61, The Life of Obstacles, section epigraph: "Love is . . ." Iris Murdoch, from the journal *The Sun*, February 2007, Issue 374, p. 48.

p. 63, The Life of Obstacles, introduction epigraph: "Pursue the obstacle . . ." written by the author. For an in-depth inquiry into obstacles as teachers, please see the chapter, "God of the Broken Tusk," in my book *Finding Inner Courage*. San Francisco, CA: Conari, 2011, p. 99.

p. 69, Ahimsikha and Angulimāla: This is my retelling of an ancient story, told to me by my friend, the storyteller Margo McLoughlin. Many other versions exist. One contemporary translation is in *The Hungry Tigress* by Rafe Martin. Boston, MA: Shambhala, 1984.

p. 103, Wu Wei's Pot: *Wu wei* is an important dynamic of Taoism, the way that gravity is essential to Newtonian physics. The literal meaning of *wu wei* is "without action" and is often embedded in the paradox *wei wu wei:* "action without action" or "effortless doing." The aim of *wu wei* is to achieve a state of whole-hearted equilibrium or alignment with the Tao, and as a result inhabit an irresistible form of soft and invisible power, the way that water, clear and soft, can erode stone and even move mountains.

p. 109, Stories of the Old World: "What's a Shiva, Grandpa . . ." In Sanskrit *Shiva* (*Śiva*) literally means *Auspicious One*. He is revered as one of the primary deities of Hinduism. *Brahma, Vishnu,* and *Shiva* each represent one of the three primary aspects of the Divine in Hinduism, known collectively as the *Trimurti*. In the Trimurti, Brahma is the creator, Vishnu is the maintainer or preserver, and Shiva is the destroyer or transformer. Shiva is often depicted with a third eye with which he burned Desire (*Kāma*) to ashes. Shiva has traditionally come to represent the dismantling of forms or habits that keep us from being reborn anew in our own lives. Though often painful, Shiva is seen as a necessary agent of Divine transformation and rebirth.

p. 113, Suffering and Loving the World, section epigraph: "My barn having burned . . ." from a Japanese card found on Phyllis Harper's dresser, as told to me by her granddaughter, Cathy McNally, in a workshop I led at Royal Roads University in Victoria, British Columbia, in April 2007.

p. 116, The Arts of Liberation: "I am alone but not alone enough . . ." from *Selected Poems of Rainer Maria Rilke,* translated by Robert Bly. NY: Harper & Row, 1981, p. 25.

p. 134, Hill Where the Lord Hides: "Commandant Jäger . . . Dr. Elkes . . ." Dr. Elkhanan Elkes was a legendary physician elected by his peers in the Kovno Ghetto in Lithuania to head the Judenrat, the Jewish Council charged with dealing with the Nazis. Judenräten were administrative bodies that the Germans required Jews to form in each ghetto in the General Government (the Nazi-occupied territory of Poland) and later in the occupied territories of the Soviet Union. These bodies were responsible for local government in the ghetto and stood between the Nazis and the ghetto population. They were forced by the Nazis to provide Jews for use as slave labor and to assist in the deportation of Jews to extermination camps. Those who refused to follow Nazi orders or were unable to cooperate fully were frequently rounded up and shot or deported to the extermination camps themselves. When the remaining Jews in the Kovno

Ghetto were sent to various concentration camps, Dr. Elkes found himself in Auschwitz under the authority of Commandant Jäger. Ordered to perform experiments on his own people, Dr. Elkes underwent a hunger strike that killed him. Part of this note is based on my own conversations with Dr. Elkes's son, Joel Elkes, a legendary physician and painter in his own right, and on Joel's book, *Dr. Elkhanan Elkes of the Kovno Ghetto: A Son's Holocaust Memoir* (MA: Paraclete Press, 1999).

p. 141, Two Monks Climb a Mountain: "Rammohun . . ." Rammohun Roy (1772–1833) was a Hindu visionary and early Universalist. Born to a prosperous Bengali family of the highest Brahman caste, he was educated in English, Persian, and Sanskrit. Studying as a young man in Patna, he began to see the common center to all paths and began to speak of this as the one All-Embracing God. Coming upon the New Testament, he fell in love with Jesus, more as a holy man than as God. Studying the Upanishads only affirmed his growing belief in the One-God-Source and that the universe is the result of one divine flow.

By the time Rammohun was an adult, he had traveled widely and added to his mastery of languages. Now he was fluent in Arabic, Hebrew, and Greek, in addition to his native Bengali and Hindi. This was highly unusual. While still in his twenties, he translated parts of the ancient texts of the Upanishads and Vedas into modern Bengali, Hindi, and English, adding his own commentaries. While he was compelled to this by the unwavering sense of unified being he found in everything he read, he was considered blasphemous for not leaving the ancient texts in their original Sanskrit.

In his late thirties, he sharpened his understanding of Hebrew and Greek in order to read the Old and New Testaments in the same way he read the Upanishads and Vedas. This led to publishing his sense of the ethical teachings of Jesus in a book called *The Precepts of Jesus.*

Though Rammohun believed in God's essential oneness, he outwardly remained a Hindu, wearing the sacred cord of an orthodox Brahman. In August of 1828, as a result of his many talks throughout the province of Bengal (one of which is depicted in this story), Rammohun founded the Brahmo Samaj, the Society of God, as a reform Hindu sect through which he could continue his conversations about the One Supreme Spirit. Rammohun died on September 27, 1833, of a fever in Bristol, Gloucestershire, England.

p. 145, Suffering and Loving the World, the story: "these warring spirits met as Angulimāla and Buddha . . ." For a more complete telling of their meeting, see the story of Ahimsikha and Angulimāla in this book (p. 69).

p. 161, The Wolf of Gubbio: Born Giovanni Francesco Bernardone, Saint Francis of Assisi (1181–1226) became the patron saint of animals and birds. There are many stories about Saint Francis and his unbridled love of animals and nature. Perhaps the most well-known is the story retold here about the wolf of Gubbio. Folklore tells us that upon meeting the wolf St. Francis said, "All these people accuse you and curse you . . . But brother wolf, I would like to make peace between you and the people." Legend has it that on his deathbed St. Francis thanked his donkey for carrying and helping him throughout his life, and his donkey wept.

p. 183, The Invitation to Grow, section epigraph: "Why is the road . . ." An old Zen story shared anonymously in a workshop I led at Omega Institute in August 2006.

p. 186, The Invitation to Grow, introduction: "Another lesson is more recent . . ." Helen Luke (1906–1996) was a Jungian analyst with remarkable clarity and grounding in the eternal mysteries. I was privileged to have Helen as a mentor toward the end of her life. For more on Helen and her insight on the inner life, please see *Such Stuff as Dreams are Made of: The Autobiography and Journals of Helen Luke*, Helen M. Luke. NY: Parabola Books, 2000.

p. 187, Tu Fu's Reappearance: Tu Fu (712–770) was a prominent Chinese poet of the Tang Dynasty. He and Li Po are frequently called the greatest of the Chinese poets. Forever linked, Tu Fu was barely known in his own time, while Li Po was widely famous. Together, they mirror other braided contemporaries such as Coleridge and Wordsworth, and Thoreau and Emerson. I first "met" Tu Fu as a young graduate student and was stunned by his immediate heart across the ages. When I was struggling through cancer, he appeared to me repeatedly in dreams as a guide. Please see Burton Watson's *The Selected Poems of Tu Fu* and Kenneth Rexroth's *One Hundred Poems from the Chinese*.

p. 215, Hands Like Wings: I want to thank the talented sculptor, Karen French-Hall. This story is based on conversations we've shared. She is the artist who gives life to the angels with large hands. About the nature of art, Karen says, "A listening heart beholds the secrets of the universe and strengthens what holds the stars apart and love intact. My work manifests from a sense of living that waits beneath these daily rites of passage."

Gratitudes

TWO MYTHIC STORYTELLERS OF MY YOUTH were my Grandmother who would sit me on her knee on that altar in Brooklyn which she called a stoop and my Great-Uncle Axi who would gather us on the floor of that small Brooklyn kitchen spinning tales of the Everglades. More recently, I am indebted to three master storytellers: Margo McLoughlin, the poet-Kora-song-praiser Kurtis Lamkin, and to Oprah Winfrey who always teaches with heart, to the heart.

I'm also grateful to my agent, Eve Atterman, for her unfailing support, and to James Munro and Fiona Baird and the WME team for their commitment through the years. And to my publicist, Eileen Duhne, for bringing me to the world. And to my former agent, Jennifer Rudolph Walsh, for her constant welcome.

To my dear friends for the story we keep weaving together. Especially George, Don, Paul, Skip, TC, David, Parker, Pam, Patti, Karen, Paula, Ellen, Dave, Jill, Jacquelyn, Linda, Michelle, Rich, Carolyn, Henk, Sandra, Elesa, Penny, Sally and Joel. And to our friend Steve, who is no longer with us. He so loved the table questions! And to Paul Bowler for the long adventure and the tender table we always come to.

About the Author

With over a million copies sold, **MARK NEPO** has moved and inspired readers and seekers all over the world with his #1 *New York Times* bestseller *The Book of Awakening*. Beloved as a poet, teacher, and storyteller, Mark has been called "one of the finest spiritual guides of our time," "a consummate storyteller," and "an eloquent spiritual teacher." His work is widely accessible and used by many and his books have been translated into more than twenty languages. A bestselling author, he has published twenty-two books and recorded fifteen audio projects. In 2015, he was given a Life-Achievement Award by AgeNation. In 2016, he was named by *Watkins: Mind Body Spirit* as one of the 100 Most Spiritually Influential Living People, and was also chosen as one of OWN's *SuperSoul 100*, a group of inspired leaders using their gifts and voices to elevate humanity. And In 2017 Mark became a regular columnist for *Spirituality & Health Magazine*.

Recent work includes *The Book of Soul* (St. Martin's Essentials, 2020); *Drinking from the River of Light* (Sounds True, 2019), a Nautilus Book Award Winner; *More Together Than Alone* (Atria,

2018) cited by *Spirituality & Practice* as one of the Best Spiritual Books of 2018; *Things That Join the Sea and the Sky* (Sounds True, 2017), a Nautilus Book Award Winner; *The Way Under the Way: The Place of True Meeting* (Sounds True, 2016), a Nautilus Book Award Winner; *The One Life We're Given* (Atria) cited by *Spirituality & Practice* as one of the Best Spiritual Books of 2016, *Inside the Miracle* (Sounds True) selected by *Spirituality & Health Magazine* as one of the top ten best books of 2015; *The Endless Practice* (Atria) cited by *Spirituality & Practice* as one of the Best Spiritual Books of 2014; and *Seven Thousand Ways to Listen* (Atria), which won the 2012 Books for a Better Life Award.

Mark was part of Oprah Winfrey's *The Life You Want Tour* in 2014 and has appeared several times with Oprah on her *Super Soul Sunday* program on OWN TV. He has also been interviewed by Robin Roberts on *Good Morning America*. *The Exquisite Risk* was listed by *Spirituality & Practice* as one of the Best Spiritual Books of 2005, calling it "one of the best books we've ever read on what it takes to live an authentic life." Mark devotes his writing and teaching to the journey of inner transformation and the life of relationship. He continues to offer readings, lectures, and retreats.

Please visit Mark at: www.MarkNepo.com, http://threeintentions.com and https://www.harrywalker.com/speakers/mark-nepo.

Permissions

E ARLIER VERSIONS OR SKETCHES OF SOME of these stories
originally appeared in editions of my other books. Thanks for
permission to reprint them in their evolved form here:

Finding Inner Courage (originally published as *Facing the Lion, Being the Lion*):
excerpt from "God of the Broken Tusk" (appears here as "The Life of Obstacles"), reworked excerpt from "Vengeance or Music" (appears here as "The Holes
of a Flute"). Copyright © 2011 by Mark Nepo. Reprinted by permission of
Conari Press.

Fire Without Witness: "Moses has Trouble with God's Instructions." Copyright ©
1988 by Mark Nepo. Reprinted by permission of British American Publishers,
Ltd.

"Hill Where the Lord Hides," from *Blood to Remember: American Poets on the Holocaust*, edited by Charles Fishman. St. Louis, Missouri: Time Being Books, 2007,
second edition, p. 305. Reprinted by permission of Time Being Books.

Inhabiting Wonder: "From Pear to Nest," "To Sprout an Ear," "Poise," "Cain and
Abel," "Blessedly." Copyright © 2004 by Mark Nepo. Reprinted by permission
of Bread for the Journey International.

Suite for the Living: "With Great Effort," "Gemseed" (a reworked version appears
here as "In the Mirror"), "Tu Fu's Reappearance." Copyright © 2004 by Mark

About Freefall Books

Throughout my life, I have been blessed to be prolific. In large part, this is because I am compelled to write about what I don't know. If I only wrote about what I know, I would have written very little. I have also been blessed to have wonderful publishers and editors over the years with whom I still work and publish. With the creation of Freefall Books, I am establishing an imprint through which I can share books that have not been able to find a home in the commercial publishing world. This imprint allows me the creative freedom to bring to you compelling roads of inquiry in books that have served as teachers for me.

I would describe the theme of Freefall Books this way: before you can fly, you have to welcome falling. It is the in between space that calls for us to open our heart and spread our wings. It is the in between space that is transformative and life-giving. For there is always a moment between falling and flying where we are most deeply instructed about life. Freefall Books is devoted to the exploration of that deeply instructive moment—however it appears—and to the covenant of care, best expressed by the Renaissance philosopher Pico Mirandola. In 1486, after writing 900 theses to explore the unity of religion, philosophy, nature, and magic, Pico concluded that "friendship is the end of all philosophy."

I am grateful to my dear friend, Brooke Warner, a writer and publisher in her own right, for her help, guidance, and company in creating this imprint. And to my oldest friend, Robert Mason, for his endless support and birdlike ability to see. And to my most intimate friend, my wife, Susan McHenry, who watered the seed of this dream many years ago.

—MN

Freefall

If you have one hour of air
and many hours to go,
you must breathe slowly.

If you have one arm's length
and many things to care for,
you must give freely.

If you have one chance to know God
and many doubts, you must
set your hseart on fire.

We are blessed.

Each day is a chance.
We have two arms.
Fear wastes air.

—MN